It Takes Star Dust
To Create A Star

It Takes Star Dust To Create A Star

Donald Rayson McGrath

Writers Club Press
New York Lincoln Shanghai

It Takes Star Dust To Create A Star

All Rights Reserved © 2002 by Donald R. McGrath

No part of this book may be reproduced or transmitted in any form or by any means, graphic, electronic, or mechanical, including photocopying, recording, taping, or by any information storage retrieval system, without the written permission of the publisher.

Writers Club Press
an imprint of iUniverse, Inc.

For information address:
iUniverse
2021 Pine Lake Road, Suite 100
Lincoln, NE 68512
www.iuniverse.com

Permissions have been granted for the following works:

Excerpts from THE JERUSALEM BIBLE, copyright © 1966 by Darton, Longman & Todd, Ltd. And Doubleday, a division of Random House, Inc. Reprinted by Permission.

Excerpt from THE NEW SECRETS OF CHARISMA, BY DOE LANG copyright © 1999 by Contemporary Books a division of McGraw-Hill Companies.

ISBN: 0-595-25096-3

Printed in the United States of America

To Mary

    Who Believed

To Lynn Gasparo

    Who Breathed Inspiration

To David McNally

    Who Encouraged Soaring

To Debby, Sean & Ryan

    Who made it Heaven on Earth

ACKNOWLEDGEMENTS

Star dust is made of even finer particles and that's inspiration, encouragement and love, and to all my brothers and sisters and extended family, thank you.

To Sharon Hadden who thirty-four years later affirmed my Epiphany that took place in the mountains of Pennsylvania, and to the "Pennies" she loved; Dolly Lisa Elliott, Denise Peays, Yvonne Tucker and Arlette Price.

My dear brother Michael McGrath, for the editing and help in his role as English Teacher for a High School that set me on the right track and the track of running: Central Catholic High School.

All the actors, actresses, directors and producers and all at Manhattan Plaza during the early years of its management, especially Dorothy Slender and Rev. Rodney Kirk.

All my co-workers at the Northwest Airlines, especially my manager, Carlton Morris who knew there was a book in that credit department clerk.

All the gang of waiters and waitresses, managers and staff at the Hilton, Hyatt, Camp Snoopy, Holiday Inn, and the Earle Brown Banquet department.

Finally, Sean and Ryan my dear sons, and Debby, my wife and dearest friend, without your love and laughter there would have been no light at all.

William Tiller of Stanford University suggests, on the basis of his research, that the intensity of the coherent group-energy field (which means a group of people on the same wavelength with the same intentions at the same time) is not the sum of the number of group members but the *Square* of the number of people in the group. In other words, the power of a group of 200 people whose energies were coherent would have the numerical value not 200 but 40,000!

> Doe Lang, The New Secrets of Charisma

CONTENTS

CHAPTER 1: A GUMP IN THE FOREST 1
CHAPTER 2: STAR DUST 7
CHAPTER 3: THE YEARS 1940–1948 16
CHAPTER 4: HAPPINESS...18
CHAPTER 5: THE YEARS 1949–1952 22
CHAPTER 6: SANCTUARY 27
CHAPTER 7: THE YEARS 1953–1956 36
CHAPTER 8: DAVID'S MYSTERY 42
CHAPTER 9: THE YEARS 1957–1967 52
CHAPTER 10: P.A.T.H. 64
CHAPTER 11: 1968 68
CHAPTER 12: GOODNIGHT LASSIE, GOODNIGHT MOM 70
CHAPTER 13: THE YEARS 1969–1974 85
CHAPTER 14: FORGET ABOUT IT 94
CHAPTER 15: THE YEARS 1975–1978 101
CHAPTER 16: STARDOM VERSUS FATHERHOOD 110
CHAPTER 17: THE YEARS 1978–1979 119
CHAPTER 18: PRAYER 124
CHAPTER 19: THE YEARS 1980–1991 136

CHAPTER 20: I NEED A MIRACLE 145
CHAPTER 21: THE YEARS 1992–2001 154
CHAPTER 22: THE PEACE AT LAST CONCERT 162
CHAPTER 23: A NEW VISION 165
CHAPTER 24: WHEN I WALK AWAY 166
APPENDIX A—A LETTER FROM A MONTGOMERY JAIL 169
APPENDIX B—POETRY 1974–2000 177
APPENDIX C—THE BOOK OF TOBIT..199
APPENDIX D—THE PEACE AT LAST CONCERT........................209

CHAPTER 1: A GUMP IN THE FOREST

JUNE 13, 1939–MARCH 3, 1940

Ah such joy to be a deer in the Forest.
 I should be thanking my God in Heaven for such
A life of gentleness, and for being a swift and beautiful animal,
 But lately I want more. I approach a
  Cave where human beings are frolicking and laughing.
   I sense something spiritual.
 I hear conversation. I sense free will, desire, passion and love.
  I hear music and poetry and most of all that sweet laughter.
There are two now. They are man and woman.
 They have no idea I am outside their window. It is dark,
  They have turned out the lights, but I see them clearly.
 They are dancing in each other's arms, they continue to laugh
   And sing and kiss.
It is a moment of choice I did not think I had.
 It is a moment of destiny. That which will happen will happen
  For I am blessed at this moment to make this choice.
   I Wonder, Should I?

It is the moment of decision.

    Yes, Dear Father, I want to become a Son of God.

I know I am a thought in Your Holy Mind,

    And will remain that for Eternity. I do want to

Experience your children's journey….

    And so therefore, I chant, "Et Introibo Ad Altare

Dei (I Go To The Altar of God)"…and it is

    Here that all decisions rest.

    I rest, and my transformation

        Has begun.

I seem to be forgetting that night

In the forest. It has been very peaceful and dark these last months.

    O my God where am I?

The moment is approaching.

    It's almost that time to become a human person.

Why did I do this? I was a Deer that just wanted to

    Seek after the Streams.

Why wasn't that enough?

    Why did I hear Laughter?

Why did I listen to the Music?

    Why did I want to Love

        And to be Loved?

Why did I want to experience

    Free Will?

I hear voices.

    They are coming from those who

    Are attending on this woman they

Will call my mother.

And where is this man they will call my father?

    He's not allowed to be in the room for my birth.

        If ever I become a father, and I did; I will be

        In the room for my children's birth,

    And I was.

I remember when I will take my 5 and 6-year-old sons down

    The Water Slide in Wisconsin at the Dells.

It is dark and we are going down the water slide,

    And they are lying on my body, and

We all hold on to each other for life.

What an adventure!
Now my mother and I are holding on
To each other for dear life.
I hope they don't name me Forrest Gump.
I want to be called, let's see…Donald,
Ah, yes, a world ruler, that's the name for me.
How will they know I want it?
Will this be my last chance for
Heavenly intervention?
I know now I am a human person
Who is taking the water slide of a
Ride from the womb of Heaven to Earth.
O God, how long will it take me to learn to pray?
My thoughts are already on diapers and how helpless
I've chosen to become.
Did I choose the right parents?
Will they realize I could have stayed a
Thought in the Mind of God
And that's where I will return?

Why didn't I stay a Deer of the Universe
    That was gentle and swift and not
        Engulfed by this Sea of Human Emotion
Into which I am swimming?
    Will they love their child?
    Will my other brothers and sisters of the world
           Recognize me,
Or will they have already forgotten they were once
      Divine;
    Yes, and that they too made their own choice
        To follow the Will of their Father in Heaven?
        Will they treat me lovingly and know that
           Every Encounter with another
    Human Person is truly a
        Holy Encounter?
That every time we say "Hi" to each other
    That it really
        Is a Holy Instant (Hi), and
When we have a "Hi" that we should
        Go gentle into that good day
With each other.

Yes, and smile and laugh with one another,
    And sometimes sing and dance with one another,
        Never forgetting that we are pleasing
  In the sight of our Creator's Mind.
The world is coming at me like the rushing darkness of that
      Wisconsin water slide.
          O my God, Reality!
Here I go. Please don't let me forget you, Father.
  ….I see light,
      I hear voices…
  "Congratulations, Mildred,
      It's a boy!"
Years later I would remember all this as I passed through
    This Earth on a Journey that was something
      Akin to a film called "Forrest Gump".
I identified with Forrest because I realized my own
    Life was really a movement through
      Life's historical events and
          Spiritual experiences.

CHAPTER 2: STAR DUST

I share with you my dear friend,
This writing so as to share my thought
That there is nothing so important
As to finding out whom we are,
And what is our function on this Earth.
So I begin my dear brother
For we are all brothers
Male and female alike
As we are all Eternal Siblings, and Children of God.
I am a Son of God.
I am not going to die.
I refuse to be sick, to feel pain, and,
I only hope that I never cause anyone else to feel pain
In body or in spirit.
I believe we are all
Knights of Existence, and Spiritual Warriors.
As both Knight and Warrior I have strapped
My Sword to my side,
And like David the King
In Psalm 45,

I desire to become a hero who can

    Cry Victory

    Over Death

    Disease

    Depression

    Sadness

    Limits

    Want

    Poverty

    Prejudice

    War

    And most of all

    Victory over Making Mistakes.

I hope you recognize me in your Dreamer Self.

I hope that I can touch your most secret spirit.

Do you understand my cry of

"Victory"

Over the World that is insane?

Do you understand that when I do cry

"Victory"

As you do that we are proclaiming

In unison that there must be

A "better way".

We have traveled our seven-story mountain

And we have reached the top and together we proclaim into

The Wind,

I am

I am as God created me

I am free

I am Spirit

I am wonderful

I am a Son of God.

I recognize you finally, my brother, and you are my brothers

Men and Women alike.

I am not ashamed to say we are all lovers and we

Are free to share anything.

I am free to share

My creations which now are only a few words for this

Journey in this Journal describing the
Mystery

That I have pierced.
This was like the Mystery that
> David the Psalmist pierced and that he reveals for us in Psalm 73.
> It is like the beauty of the word that
> Solomon shares with us in his "Song of Songs"
It is like the inspiration that comes to all of us through the
> Holy writings, from The Bible to the Koran to
> "A Course in Miracles".
Also from the poetry and prose of all the ages, from Ramayana and
> Gilgamesh to Walt Whitman, and all the
> > Writers I have truly loved including Homer,
William Shakespeare, Yeats, Dostoyevsky, Abraham Lincoln,
J.K. Rowling, Mark Helprin, Richard Bach and Marianne Williamson.
> And from speeches and interviews of some of
> > The most wonderful people of our times, including
Martin Luther King, Jr., John and Robert Kennedy
> Princess Di and Mother Teresa.
> > Filled with this inspiration of my

Blessed brothers and sisters and eternal peace makers
    I journey out to gaze at the starry heavens
        And ask their Blessing on our new
            Relationship of writer and reader.
We help each other find the inspiration and the desire to
    Pierce our own Mystery. Mine is clear, my happiness
        Is assured, and as I move through this life,
I find I create the star dust that will eventually form
        A star I will journey to on my
            Way to my Heavenly home.
I have shared with you that I knew the moment of
        My conception and that I chose my parents, and
            I also share with you that I will walk
        Away from this world on March 2, 2033.
How do I know that? I know that like I know that each
        Day is just a temporary walk on the Path of Light
        That leads me from this world to my
    Eternal home. I know that because
I have pierced a Mystery that enables me to
        Walk in Light in the day and in the night,

And experience the wonder of
Discovering that this understanding is open to all of us
As Sons of God.
It is my belief that it takes star dust to create a star, and
It is in the traveling to that Star that enables me
to live in Light and to have a vision of Eternity.
This is the Light that clothes me by Day and Night, even
When it's cloudy and dark, even when my eyes
Are closed. This is the Light that comes
From being touched by the Experience of the
Mystery of God.
These are episodes of light and this experience of piercing
The mystery is so hard to share. I know that you
Hold your own mysteries in your heart and that you
Too go to your own altar and that you alone build
You're own church where in you accept your own
Followers and friends to share this Journey of a Lifetime.
So, I share my travels and discoveries with
You and I make this Act of faith—I am not going to die.
I, however, must accept that many are going to say,

"Yes you are going to die." So I admit to them that I am going
    To D.I.E. and silently accept that yes, I am going to
        Dance Into Eternity.
My brother Michael once asked me "must we always smile?"
    My answer is yes; we most not stop smiling. I do not want to
        Stop smiling, laughing, singing, dancing, praising
            And living as a Son of God.
My problem is that sometimes I forget that I am a
    Son of God
        And I choose sadness, meanness, and simply
            Being human and ordinary over
Accepting how wonderful and divine I really am.
    So, yes I am going to Dance Into Eternity, but
        I am not going to die.
How can I prove that all this is going to happen?
    I believe your visions are bolder than mine are,
        I believe you have gone beyond my imagination.
I believe you have remembered things from our eternal
    Beginnings that you have shared with no one.

Secrets that you have written over and over again
On the pages of the Book of Your Heart.
Thoughts of your very own being that may never be
Shared with anyone but you and your Self.
So do I need more proof than the inner stirrings of
Your heart that cries, "Go for it Don, be Victorious."
I am taking this moment, this Holy Instant that we share together,
To proclaim a glorious decision on my part to live in
The Now, to Love and to speak of only Blessings.
I make atonement for my meanness that I fall into by being led
Into the temptation of making mistakes and not
Doing the right thing.
That is not sin, I know no sin, and I banish
The word forever from my vocabulary.
It has caused too much pain in this world. Speaking
Of this world, I am in it, but not of it.

I repeat, I am in this World but not of this World.
> I see pain, but I accept it is not for me except
>> For the sadness which I bring on
>
> Myself when I feel any less worthy than the
>> Magnificent co-creator I am.
>
> I see sickness, but I believe I was born to live
>> Only in Health and Holiness.
>
> I see the world, but my Happiness comes from that fact
>> That I must save the world from what I thought
>>> It was.

I hope you can join me.
> I want you to go to your own altar and say,

"Introibo ad altare Dei,
>> Ad Deum qui laetificat
>
> Juventutem meam"—"I will go to the altar of God,
>> To God the Joy of my Youth."

CHAPTER 3: THE YEARS 1940–1948

I remember Grandma, and a galvanized washing tub
And that she bathed me. I remember that
I just wanted to play, play, play. No cares,
No worries, warm hugs, kisses, loving parents,
My choice of Daniel and Mildred, and my
Siblings up to now, Mickey, Danny and
Mary I love it. I love Rascal and her
Puppies. I love that Mom
Isn't upset over all the cereals and flour
All over the floor that I managed to
Pillage while she was at the store.
I love that I live only a block or so from where
Stephen Foster, Songwriter, was born.
Why is it that he will follow
Me with his music the rest of
My life right up to my final
Peace at Last Concert
In 2033?
My mother once told me that the happiest moment of her
Life was when I was conceived in the

Mountains of Pennsylvania, near Ligonier. I already knew that
But I didn't tell her. Now as a child I am aware that it's
Not happy anymore, and she is gone, and Dad has
Chosen a new Mom for me and I have a new
Younger brother, Michael.
Mom has gone off and married a Chief
In the Navy, and I also have a new
Younger sister, Barbara.
The pain of their anger and mistakes and final separation
Is forgiven and forgotten. My new mother brought
A son to the marriage also, so Jim joined us and made seven.
That was the blessing—a bigger family.
I want to love all my brothers and sisters of
The world the way I love my siblings.
I know it's just the age of reason, and for some strange
Reason I don't want to forget my God.
I know what I have to do.
I will become an altar boy.

CHAPTER 4: HAPPINESS

Where were you when you were 9 or 10 years old at 6 a.m.?
Maybe you were still sleeping or just getting
Up for school? I was already up at St. Kieran's
Church turning on the lights, lighting the
Candles, running over to the priest
House to make sure young
Father McBride was up, running back and
Costuming myself in black cassock
And white surplice, filling the water and wine
And with a turn to make sure no one was looking,
Licking a little spilt wine off my fingers.
We were ready and we began the daily Mass in
Latin with Father McBride saying:
Introibo ad altari Dei
(I go to the Altar of God)
And I responding,
Ad Deum qui laetificat juventutem mean
(To God the joy of my youth.)
I was answering for the adults in the pews,
I was answering for all the church

Faithful all over the world, sleeping and just beginning
    Their workday.
I was washing the hands of the priest who would soon turn
    Bread and wine into the Body and Blood of Christ.
    As early as 8 years old I was
Assisting in this great drama. I had become
    A young diaconate, a young servant of the
People and I would want to be one all the days of my life.
    Over age 60 I serve people food at Hotel Banquets at the
Hilton and the Hyatt and Mall of America for my part time job, and they
    Smile because I smile and I am there to see that they enjoy.
    In those moments as an altarboy, there was a
    Memory of Eternity, and an overwhelming
    Awareness that I was blessed as a child of the
Heavenly Father. As when I had been a Deer there was the
    Knowledge that I was part of a heavenly Mind,
    And that I was being chosen to taste of the
Spiritual and it filled by young being and I would
    Never lose the desire to be truly helpful.

Are you remembering your childhood? I hope you are.
Part of our extraordinary Journey together is that
You begin to Remember those instances that will
Take you back to the womb; to the first moment of your conception; and,
Yes perhaps to before that joining of a man and woman to
Bring you onto to this earth.
I have gone back to Remember and I continue to do
So, but it's such a slow process. I remember
That I once thought I had been Alexander the Great's horse, Bucephalus.
It took place in the midst of running and jumping over hedges back
And forth along a beautiful block surrounding the Cathedral at the
University of Pittsburgh. It was an incredible flashback, and I can
Not be sure, that just maybe this was a life prior to
Becoming a Deer in the woods of Pennsylvania, but
That is not as certain in my mind yet, as the
Moment of conception I have shared
With you.
This recalling to Mind when you were in the Mind of God and
When you were pure Thought is something you must
Discover for yourself. I know we get a hint of it
When we have an experience that moves

Us and we are overcome by inexplicable Happiness, and
A very clear Voice whispering "This is truly about
Your Self—You have pierced the Mystery"
When I pierced that Mystery,
I understood the object of my journey and that was Happiness.
I was more than just an 8 to 12 year old altar boy answering the
Priest for the People. I was chosen to use my
Voice—the Voice for God through me was the Will of my
Father. I was chosen to be a co-creator and to be creative.
These words have been inscribed on my heart all the days of my life;
"We must proceed as men and women as though
Limits to our Abilities do not exist, We are collaborators in Creation."
(Attributed to Pierre Teilhard de Chardin)
I knew at that age that I was chosen to be a Co-Creator, Father,
An Actor, Singer of Songs, and a Master of
Ceremonies, a Writer/Lecturer, a Loving Voice for Peace in this World, a
And most of all, a creator of Star Dust.
I want to remember all the days of my life that the Heavenly Mind is Every Mind
Extending itself and asking for recognition. When all is said and done,
There will be nothing left for all of us except
Happiness and to spend Eternity Together.

CHAPTER 5: THE YEARS 1949–1952

I am also a paper boy. I love this world in the
Morning since it's so delightful to be out alone.
I like the sound of my rolled-up
Post-Gazette hitting against the front doors. I have made such
Wonderful adult friends. When I collect money from
Them on Saturday, they give me tips, and coffee
Cake and sometimes the forbidden—coffee.
But most importantly what they really give me is continual
Praise for being so industrious as a young age. They
Realize that I am also their deliverer for the
Evening papers, The Pittsburgh Press and
The Sun-Telegraph. They
Congratulate me on the new
3 cent postage stamp just issued:
"In recognition of the important service rendered their
Communities and their nation by America's newspaper boys."
On holidays I am really dedicated, because the
Evening papers do not publish and you can
Volunteer to hawk the special
Edition put out by the morning paper.

So while folks are sleeping I
    Am walking up and down the streets yelling
        At the top of my voice, "Post-Gazette
            Morning Paper, the only paper out
                Today."
I often wondered why no one yells at me—"shut up
    Kid, we're trying to sleep." Instead they tip
        Grandly and even ask,
            "Are you the one
    Who goes by in the early morning singing?
"Mocking Bird" and "Down by the
Riverside?" They are right, it's me and I love singing the
    Songs of the 4 Lads, 4 Aces, the Mills Brothers,
        Patti Page, Kay Starr, Johnny Ray, Jo
Stafford, the Hilltoppers, and of course, Doris Day.
"What will be will be" touches this little
Gump from the Forest, because I know it's part of
    Beginning to understand the Mystery. There
        Are temptations to do the wrong thing?
            And to forget, and to be mean and

Act like a brute and make one mistake after another.
But I keep trying to Remember.
I remember Mama and how she cries when I
Finish our Sunday Afternoon visit at her
New apartment in Shadyside.
She Holds me close and calls me her
Baby and I cry with her. When I get home Dad
Wants to know if I had a good time. "It
Was great", I say smiling, but my father is
Not smiling. He is upset I am so happy.
"Well go live with her if that's what you want?" I am ten and
Now I know what confusion is for the first time. "May
I go to bed, Dad?" "No, you want to be with her,
Pack your things and get out." I walk
Upstairs and stare at my dresser. I finally figure it out.
I pack one tee shirt folded inside one
Pair of short pants and go back
Downstairs just hoping Dad will be done with this.
Goodbye, he says, and I leave home packed and not knowing
Where to go. I stand out at the streetcar stop not knowing

If it was a streetcar or a bus that we took on the visits.
    It's snowing and I shiver, but my thoughts are
        A prayer, "Mom, if I knew how to get
           To you tonight, I'd come, but
              I don't know what to do."
Dad is behind me and calls me and takes my
    Hand, "Come home to bed, son, he says,
        And holding his hand I cry that
For a moment I almost deserted him, and
    I happily go off to bed.
        In the morning as with all of our family,
There is never a mention of the past.
    It's forgotten, it's forgiven and it's a new day.
It's great growing up, and I find myself
    Enjoying Saturday matinees and
Now at 12 falling in love with the most beautiful
    Irish-Polish girl in the neighborhood.
It would take me 10 years to get over her, but she gave me
    A feeling of warmth at all times in her presence.
Like my very first attraction in kindergarten

At St. Paul's in Carnegie, Pa, I was always to
Be smitten by a glance. Gigi was
Beauty, and Solomon speaks of
That glance that comes from a woman of bliss. Today
As in the heart of a small child, I continue to
Sing the "Song of Songs" and it takes me on a
Dance of memories that are always with me.
I liked the road in the forest I was taking.
I loved what Love was doing to my
Body and my soul. I knelt in meditation at
12 years old and I remember what I repeated
Over and over,
"Let me always love a beautiful woman,
"Let me be a good father, and above all,
Let me be close to them and
Make them happy.

CHAPTER 6: SANCTUARY

Children and teenagers, do I dare try to discuss them?
   Well, I am a proud father who has run the
      Gauntlet of parenthood, along with a
         Wonderful wife Debby, who has been an incredible
            Mother.
As parents we all share the joy and the sadness of raising
   Our beautiful children and at times it's tough.
There are the happy wonder years, and then there are the
   Years the darlings of our lives dare us to try and
      Interfere with theirs. The hugs of dear
Childhood become memories during their transition from
   Childhood to adulthood and the mysterious
      Experience of that incredible Journey.
We as parents and collaborators in creation, do
   Everything we can to protect this unbelievable
      Co-creation with our Heavenly Father/Mother.
Jesus sent the disciples to care for the sick and to cast
   Out demons. We also go two by two, and we choose
      The partner that we love and that we know
         Will care and protect the children.

This partner must have no other requirements than
A commitment to go to the Altar of God each
Day and swear they will try to find the
Best way for child raising. The
Children must not be punished by our mistakes
And our partner of love must remember.
Remember the journey back to their own childhood and
Possibly back even further. It is possible they may
Even hear the ancient melodies and have
Memories of what their child hearts
Cried out for as they hoped for tenderness and that
Their protectors did all they could do to
Give them lives as close to Paradise as
They could.
We must not punish children as adults and penalize
Them for what society have wrought. They
Are now guilty of adult crimes and
As they come before the Tribunal of Loving Kindness,
There must not be a rush to judgment and a
Miscarriage of Justice. We must ask, and
Ask again:

Why are they acting the way they are?
    Why are they turning to murderous acts
        In this our twenty-first century?
Prepare yourselves for this answer because I have
    Thrown myself on the ground of mystery and ask the
        Sphinx for an answer.
            The Sphinx answered:
                "Your children are
                Afraid, and most violent
                Acts are committed out of
                Fear. Your children are afraid."
My dear siblings of the world our children are afraid.
    They are no longer loved, protected and held sacred.
        They are beaten, raped, abducted…they are
            Fought over in courts…they are used
                For revenge, profit, illicit
                    Pleasures, and even
                        Sacrifice.
How can we begin to help them?
    We must remove Fear and above all we must
        First remove Fear from our lives.

The Master Teacher of the Sermon on the Mount
    Suggests it would be better to be drowned
        In the depths of the sea with a great
            Millstone around the neck,
Than to scandalize the children. He wanted to
    Protect them and was asking that they
        Be given Sanctuary.
Do not scandalize the children of the world, do not
    Starve them, do not give them weapons, and do not
        Ask them to fight wars or have sex, and
            Do not tear them out of the arms of
                Their loving protectors.
    They have Sanctuary.
Now we have a problem, for we have to punish our
    Children for becoming drug addicts, drug pushers,
        Haters of parents, society, humanity, and
            Finally for becoming killers.
We must forgive them, and we must learn how to forgive
    The world its mistakes, but first we must forgive the
                Children.
    In order to do this we must speed up the return of

Love for the Children of the World.
　　We must feed them, protect them, and keep
　　　　Them from feeling unsafe in our world.
We must give them a garden to play, rest and grow in
　　While growing up in our world.
We must do the right thing and forgive those who have
　　Broken the law because they acted our of the
Fear of living in our society. We must put our arms around
　　Them as we may have to put some kind of fences
　　　　Around them. This will protect them and
　　　　　　Protect those they are trying to
　　　　　　　　Harm.
We will have a chance to teach them, but they will also be able to
　　Teach us: What did we do wrong?
　　　　We must do the right thing. We must as
　　　　　　Citizens of the world return to an
　　　　　　　　Ancient idea: Ask the Village
　　　　　　　　　　To love our children.
We cry out now and till the end of time, "Love the Children".
　　They are not to be hit or hurt by anyone. Their
　　　　Parents, step-parents, grandparents, guardians

Teachers, ministers and politicians must protect them from
    All those who want to hurt them. The Village, so
  Beautifully described in the African work, and reinforced
      Recently by Hillary Clinton, must surround them with the
Laws, programs, education, support and inspiration
    That they require as Children of God.
Yes, we care about the forests and the trees, and all
    The endangered species for they are also creations
      We protect. And, we are not here to pollute our
  Streams and oceans. However, it is a most important
      Goal to come together as one World and agree
        To give the children Sanctuary, which
Is a return to holiness and joy in the Journey they are undertaking.
    Let them not fear to walk this earth with us.
As I shared with you my early years of rising from bed and
    Walking down a dark street into an unlit church, only
      To be the one to turn the lights on and to light
        The candles of worship, and doing so
Without fear. Let all the children of the world
    Be permitted to walk in the dark and feel safe
      And to be restored in the knowledge
        That they are children of light and that they will

Bring with them the Light of the World.
We join our prayers at night with those shining stars of
Etan and Sara from New York, and Jacob from
Minnesota that there will never be a child
Abducted again. That children with be protected by the
Angels and by us and given the foundations of
Confidence and Trust to want to
Walk happily into their teen years.
To all teenagers I say never forget you are at all times our
Hope and our future. Do the right thing even when
Others are not. Above all listen. Listen to
That inner voice that will reveal to you the
Path you are going to take on this wonderful
Journey.
Be aware of the interest you have during your teen years,
Because they are hints of what you should choose to fill
Your lives with joy. Those appetites and interests,
Will stir your creative thoughts and direct your leisure times, to a
Foundation for a life of happiness in your adulthood.
Listen, be aware, and recognize your Creative Self and involve
That Self where the Spirit of your Life is trying to guide

You. Be assured that Voice can be heard
And only by you. Involve yourself, dedicate yourself,
Enjoy yourself, and dance, sing, love your world of
Activity, studies, friendships and most importantly
Your discoveries. Pursue your lifetime
Of happiness on your journey Home!
Every time you hear that criticism that your heads are in the
Clouds or your feet don't touch the ground,
Smile. Maybe that's just the perfect
Definition of a teenager.
You who are the builders of the world of
Tomorrow, are in the world, but not of it. This is exactly
What us adults who are stumbling have forgotten.
That is our tragic flaw as adults that we have
Forgotten who we are, who we were, who we are to become,
What we are here for, and where we are going.
You are the next generation of the protectors of
The Children. Get over your fears that we
Have tried to instill in you and work for peace in the
Village. Establish Sanctuary for the little ones,
And build a new

    Garden of Responsibility while
Creating a universe we all
        Dreamed about but
    Really didn't believe in.
        Believe in it.
Remember, listen and above all don't forget:
    We are all depending on you.

CHAPTER 7: THE YEARS 1953–1956

They were wonder years those first twelve and
It was with becoming a teenager that happiness
    Came with standing and singing on the
        Corners of my new neighborhood,
            Morningside.
The girls from St. Raphael High School made the
    Boys from Central Catholic High School very
        Happy by dancing with us to the romantic
            Tunes of the Hilltoppers, Four Freshman,
              Four Coins, the Penguins, and
              Most of all, Johnny Mathias.
        The fast songs were great with rock and
    roll and rhythm and blues and rock around the clock
        Bill Haley to Red Prysock, who allowed
Janice Cirincione and I to stop the crowd
        While they cheered us on. Dancing was an
A beautiful addiction. It began my
Dance Into Eternity that has never ceased, and
        It's funny that even as a deer it was
            That very thing that attracted

Me so much to my mother and father.
Walking and running became a way
Of life. I was a cross-country runner
And today I continue to be a marathoner. I walked
Miles to work as a caddy and then walked all
Day on a beautiful golf course in Fox Chapel.
Summers were more work than play now that I had
Become a teenager. It was never again going
To be simply summers of play as it was as a child. I had
Aunt Edna, Uncle Joe and Aunt Vi all Summer and
They were the kind of relatives that make
You feel warm all over whenever you recall them
To mind.
The love of mornings from altarboy to paperboy to caddy
To running at dawn was a love of the Journey. I was
Happiest when I was moving. My nights were
To be used for dancing and singing
And happiness was a word called
Theatre. I had been singing on the corner and
At dances with Scotty, Bob Limpert, Bob Regal, Rich Hughes,
Ralph Watson and Paul Dewey.

Bobby Regal talked me into auditioning for the
Central High School Musicals and I
Played leads in Carousel and The
King and I. My director was
A member of a teaching order. Brother Theodore who
Believed we should be professionals and what an
Experience. Years later on Broadway I saw
What he saw for us. I continue to sing the songs of the musicals
Everyday and it makes life grand. I had a woman
In my life and at 92 years old she is still my
Love. Bobby Regal had a great family
And his sister Charlotte became a best friend. His mom,
Mrs. Regal, had the most wonderful home to
Visit. You had to eat and it didn't matter
If you were hungry or not, you ate.
All night long she would have visitors and
Just sitting around her table was a joy. She and her
Husband Charlie always-demanded songs from
The musicals and you thought you were
Performing at Carnegie Hall. Mrs. Regal treated
All the guys like they were her own boys
And her love for us was a treasure

Today at 92 and healthy she stands on the porch and
    I run the steps as though I was still a
        Teen. She still calls me Joe Clown
A nickname I received because I like to
        Make people laugh. What I did not
Like is that kids thought they could
        Take your name and make fun of it.
        I felt that when we
Made fun of someone, or called them names,
We forgot our God, our Origins, our Creation, and
    Especially our Relationship with all of our
        Brothers and Sisters of the earth.
I always suffered when others were being criticized
    Or ridiculed and it was surprising that I
        Was to be led into hurting someone
        I cared for by my stupidity.
His name was Doc Robin and he was the owner
    Of our Morningside Drug Store. It was a
        Warm place for a teen. Soda, candy
    Cigs and companionship. Doc and Mrs. Robin
        And their daughter Sheila were the warmest
        Jewish family on the block.

The Robins family let us "hang out" with dignity and
                Only asked that we behave while we were in the
                        Store sitting at the soda fountain.
We stood outside talking to one another as friends. Older boys
        With "souped up" cars used Doc's as a meeting place.
One night one of them said that if I really wanted to see
                Doc laugh at me I should go in the store and do a
                        "Heil Hitler."
                Thinking I'd be funny in my role as Joe Clown, I did.
Doc came right up over the counter in a single bound like a
                Lion escaping from a cage. I bolted out the
Door and he chased me for a mile.
                I was fast, but if Doc wasn't wearing those
                        Spade shoes of the 50's, I think he
                                Would have caught me.
I returned the next day when the store was empty except for
                Doc. "I am so sorry Doc, I said." He response was
                        So memorable. "It's okay Joe, I know you
                Would have never done that unless you were put up to it.
Always think first and you will always do the right thing,

Never let others intimidate you into action
> You really don't want to do. Never let
>> Others live your life for you."
I never forgot the advice, and his
> Forgiveness was like
Oil down Aaron's beard.
> Hey Doc, thanks.

CHAPTER 8: DAVID'S MYSTERY

How good, how delightful it is
    For all to live together like brothers;
Fine as oil on the beard,
    Running down the beard,
Running down Aaron's beard
    To the collar of his robes;
Copious as the morning dew
    Falling on the heights of the mountains,
When Yahweh confers his blessing of
        Everlasting Life.
            (Psalm 133)

I continue to share with you my dear friend the
    Dearest discoveries of a lifetime. There is
        Nothing like the discovery of great books,
            And the blessings that come from the
        Discoveries of the greatest writings of all time,
            As well as the most spiritual writings of
                All time.
    The journey started with an eight-year-old who walked
        A mile of Lawrenceville streets and hills
    From the library with 10 books under his arms.

It continued through attending Duquesne University in
>> Pittsburgh and meeting Dr. William G. Storey.
He led us college students in the chanting of the
>> Psalms using his own work,
>>> "Morning Praise and Evensong" and
I have never ceased in my living with the
>> Power and the beauty of the Psalms.
I discovered the Psalms were called the
>> Prayer of the Church and that
Holy men and women of the Christian world and
>> Rabbi's and teachers of the
>>> Jewish world prayed them
Continuously throughout the ages
>> Ever since their creation by
David of the Old Testament.
>> A dear friend of Del and Carol Rayson,
>> My mother and father in law,
Kathleen Norris, continues with her loving works to
>> Bring people to the psalms that continue to be
>>> Offered by many as a Universal Prayer of
>>>> Peace and brotherhood. I have read

Many translations of the Psalms,
    But none more excellent than the
Jerusalem Bible, 1966 edition by Doubleday.
In March 2000 it was once again made available.
    Thank you Doubleday!
        Psalms transform and
    Bless the reader. They console,
Inspire and elevate the reader to the Mystery of spirituality
    Simply because they allow one's own interpretation.
    I also have re-written them, because I find no
Need to include the vengeful, spiteful, hateful mention of
    Enemies and sinners. I feel that everyone that
    Touches them is touched by a mystery.
Psalm 73 reveals that David is touched by the
    Mystery. He tells us, "I have
    Penetrated the Mystery and I have discovered that
    I have been acting like a brute."
He, as well as we, can discover the Mystery of the
Experience of Divine Thought. We can like David penetrate the
    Mystery of the Experience of God.
I had penetrated the Mystery and now I wanted to correct
    Mistakes I had made in my life and went humbly

Before the Altar of God and asked,
> "How have I acted the Brute?

How do I return to the gentle ways of loving and
> Forgiving? How do I live forgiving even
>> Myself, letting the past go without
>>> Worry about the future, and Living in the Now?"

Hopefully you will see how the next forty years was a journey
> That tried to answer those questions. I had begun on a
>> Journey and the 150/151 Psalms filled by days

As I tried to penetrate the Mystery of My Life. I went
> Before the Altar of God now knowing I was
>> No less than a Son of God, and only
>>> A little less than the Angels.

I had been a deer in the forest and heard:

> *As the deer searches for the stream*
>> *So my soul is searching for you my God.*
>>> *(Psalm 42)*

I wanted to live in the City of God and know that
> I was always to go to the river for inspiration.

There is a River whose streams refresh the
> *City of God, and it sanctifies the*

Dwelling of the Most High. (Psalm 46)
I had found the Shepherd in the
Psalms that would care for the
Lambs of the Universe.
You anoint my head with oil,
My cup brims over. Ah, how
Goodness and kindness pursue me.
(Psalm 23)

I actually ran with the Psalms in my heart, and even in the ice and snow
I found I would stumble but never fall.
No disaster can overtake you,
No plague comes near your tent:
He will put you in his angel's charge
To guard you wherever you go.
They will support you on their hands
In case you hurt your foot against a stone.
(Psalm 91)

I continued to sing and realize how wonderful it was to be a
Knight of Existence battling windmills with my good
Friend Don Quixote. I realized I was among
Brothers and Sisters of the world who were all
Holy and who all were

Priests in one way or another.
Royal dignity was yours from day you were born,
    On the holy mountains,
Royal from the womb, from the dawn
    Of your earliest days.
Yahweh has sworn an oath which he never will retract,
    "You are a priest of the order of Melchizdeck,
        Forever and forever.
        (Psalm 110)

My heart was now stirred by a noble theme. I
    Saw the hero and the heroine in society
        Always working for Peace. I strove
To be a hero also, for in that striving we discover
    We are more than just myths, but we are
        The answer to a weary world. I would
Run like the first marathoner of Greece and
    Always cry out, "Victory".
My heart is stirred by a noble theme:
    Hero, strap your sword at your side,
In majesty and splendor, ride on,
    In the cause of truth

<u>This is why God, has anointed you</u>
With the oil of gladness.
(Psalm 45)

I repeat what I said earlier. I went before the altar of
God now knowing I was no less than a Son of
God, and only a little less than the Angels.

What is the son of man that you should care for him?
You have made him little less than the angels,
You have crowned him with glory and splendor.
(Psalm 8)

I now felt like a spiritual warrior who along with
David the Psalmist would strap my sword to my
Side to proclaim Victory and Peace at Last.
I would sing with Praise with the Brides and the Bridegrooms
All children sitting around the table of life growing in
Forgiveness, acceptance and love.
Children are a bounty from Yahweh,
He rewards with descendents:
Like arrows in a hero's hand
Are children.
Happy are the caretakers who fill their quiver

With arrows of this sort.
Happy are those who Love Yahweh
    And follow Yahweh's Path
Your love and your children: fruitful vines
    On the inner walls of your house.
Your love and your children: round your table
    Like shoots round an olive tree.
        (Psalms 127 and 128)

I was born to sing and dance and to celebrate, to stand
    By the rivers of the world, and cry war no more and
        Peace at Last. I would now beat the drums,
    Blow the trumpets and join in an
Universal shout to vibrate the planets, make the stars burn
    More brightly and do my individual best to
        Spread star dust all over the place.
Praise with blasts of trumpets,
    Praise with lyre and harp,
Praise with drums and dancing,
    Praise with strings and reeds,
Praise with clashing cymbals.
    Let everything that breathes:

Praise Transcendent Greatness!
(Psalm 150)

I walk the Lawns outside the Gates of Heaven. I know where
I am going, I understand now, and daily I go
   To the altar and share with all those who
      Go there and Listen and penetrate
         The Mystery of Life.

I tried to analyze the problem,
   Hard though I found it—
Until the day I pierced the mystery
   When my heart was growing sour
With pains shooting through my loins,
   I had simply failed to understand
My stupid attitude to you was brutish.
   Even so, I stayed in your presence,
You held my right hand;
   Now guide me with your advice
And in the end receive me into glory.
         (Psalm 73)

Send out your light and your truth,
   Let these be my guide,
To lead me to your Holy Mountain

And to the place where you live.
Then I shall go to the altar of God,
To the God of my Youth and Joy.
(Psalm 43)

CHAPTER 9: THE YEARS 1957–1967

It is nearing graduation from Central Catholic
    High School in Pittsburgh. I have no
        Idea what I should do. There's no money to
Go to college, and I know I would just clown around the way
    I have been doing for the last couple of years. I got
        Good grades, but I was always performing, and
Especially looking to make folks laugh. I danced and dated and
    Thought the Senior Year of High School was
        Incredible. The good friends of Morningside
And from the Musicals at the school were just terrific. I sang
The romantic leads in "Carousel" and "The King and I"
    And couldn't believe how special it was to be applauded.
I started to work for All State Insurance Company and
    After only two months works I wanted something
        Different. I traveled to work on the old
Fashioned street cars, that ran down cobble stone
    Streets. I remember the very day watching
Out the window I thought to myself, "I could be doing this
    For the next 50 years, so what's 3 or 4 away in the
        Service." I chose the U.S. Navy and went

On a kitty cruise, as they called it if you were
   Only 17 years old when you joined, that
Was to be a wonderful experience. I was sent to
Work with NATO headquarters in Naples, Italy in a small
   Town called Bagnoli. I had my own car, a laundry
      Business and I was to join the International
Theatre group and do eight theatrical productions over
   The next two years. A friend, Terry Fockler, asked
Me once, was I going to go to New York after I left the Navy.
   I didn't even fathom that I could possibly be an
      Actor as a profession. I enjoyed it, I was good,
I found I loved making people cry as well as laugh, but a
   Real actor, it just was too far-fetched. I love the
      Theatre, my small town outside Naples, my dear
         Best friend, Danny Bender, who was to remain
So for forty years, and most of all I loved the people, and
   Sharing food and wine with the Italians. I traveled
      To Capri, Sorrento, Rome, and all over Europe,
   Forgetting that I was actually from Pittsburgh, Pa. And
      That someday I might have to return there.

I thought about the Priesthood, but it wasn't until
I went to a retreat in Sorrento with an
American priest who was with the
Franciscans at the Vatican. I told him I was
Puzzled about my vocation. "What would you really like
To do," he asked. I want to be a father with a bunch
Of kids, I replied. "I don't recommend the Priesthood, Father
Shannon said, and listen to your heart and how
Happy and with what passion you say you want family."
We stayed in touch for years, and I always thought of him
As the person who allowed me to verbalize for the
First time, what I was supposed to do in life.
I visited Assisi and prayed to St. Francis, to Padua and prayed
To St. Anthony not to return until 40 years later with my
Family. I had an audience with the wonderful Pope John XXIII and I
Traveled to San Giovanni Rotondo in Foggia, Italy to kiss
The hands of the famous priest of Italy, Padre Pio.
At the Mass he took off his gloves and revealed that
He really did have the Stigmata like St. Francis.
I was never bashful so I went to the priest house and said
An American Sailor very much

Wanted to meet him. He allowed me to
    Visit with him and kneel at his feet and kiss
        His sacred hands. I left inspired with
A thought. The remembrance of that kiss will be
    With me all the days of my life.
I felt I would always be like him, and like St. Francis
        Of Assisi, and that of being a Teacher of Peace.
Had they paid American sailors to stay in Italy,
        And walk around in a brown robe, I believe
            I would have applied for the position.
When you are in Assisi you feel as though you have
        Gone back in time and that the teachings of
            This beautiful saint and lover of peace,
        Francis permeated the countryside. I used to
            Think if only peace like this could permeate
        The entire world.
I almost stayed in the Navy and shipped for six more
    Years as the expression goes, but something
        Inside was hinting to me that it was now
    Time to go and get and education.
I returned to Pittsburgh and Duquesne University.

On my last night before returning I was walking
    Under the stars in Rome I threw a coin in
        The Fountain di Trevi and wished I
Would return some day, but as I looked up
    To the stars I began to understand
That I yearned to be shining down rather than
    Looking up. I realized I was so close
        To my Father in Heaven and
That a wonderful Journey to the stars and to
    Him was in store for me.
I didn't know what to be, I studied and I thought
    Maybe I should teach little children since
        I love them so, but I could not
Come to a decision what to be. I chose to major
    In philosophy and minor in theology, so
        That I could finally have an answer
            When I was asked that question
What was I going to do? I always had one answer
    Which was I was going to be happy.
Duquesne University was exciting and I worked my way
    Through the first two years by putting six nights a week

At the Pittsburgh Post Office. I saved enough money so
Now I could work fun jobs, join and preside over
Student organizations, and become totally
Involved in University life.
I became President of the Chi Rho Society.
Time magazine was to report in 1971 that the
Catholic Charismatics had their humble
Beginnings with that small group of
Students from Duquesne
University. It was a joy to be so spiritually close
To so many wonderful men and women.
I took a job and became a secretary for Dr. William G. Storey, who
Published a beautiful anthology, "The Days of our Lord".
He is also the editor of "Day by Day—a Notre Dame Prayer Book"
Still used by many college and high school students.
I also was an assistant to a hero. His name was
Father H. A. Rheinhold and he escaped from the wrath of
Hitler since he was an outspoken Navy Chaplain.
He fled to Switzerland and then to America.
His books on the Liturgy, especially

"Bringing the Mass to the People",
    Were very instrumental in the format for the Liturgical
Changes that came out of Vatican II. He had
    Parkisons disease, and struggled every
Night to transcribe his articles, the book he was writing
    For Herder & Herder press and answering the
    Mail that still came daily from all over
    The world. He was my hero and
I loved bathing him. I massaged his body for an hour after
    The bath. One night Fr. Rheinhold said to me,
"God really loves me. Here an old broken down Navy
    Chaplain is sent a young ex-sailor to make him
    Feel young every night before going off to sleep."
I was also President of the Interracial Society and I
    Was a young democrat who was able to
    Escort Hubert Humphrey around the
    City when he passed through Pittsburgh
    On his political journey.
I loved following whatever Martin Luther King, Jr., John F.
    Kennedy and Robert F. Kennedy were
    Doing. I was devastated at John's death. I traveled
    To Washington, DC, to see John-John salute

His father with my good friend Bob Limpert. I
    Walked the streets of Washington and I
        Cried. John was gone.
I continued to study and sing the Psalms at the
    Morning meetings of the Chi Rho Society.
I continued to join with a minority of students to
    Bring speakers to the school that spoke
        About spiritual topics or race relations.
It was my senior year when the Selma March was broadcast
    Over the TV, in March of 1965. I left with busloads
        Of university students to join with the people
        Of the south that they were not to
    Be persecuted and beaten in front of TV
        Cameras, because they wanted to
            Vote.
I have a letter I wrote from Montgomery Jail in the midst of
    A hunger strike. (Appendix A)
        But what I did not say was that I thought
            Deep in my heart, that this choice to
        Demonstrate was probably my last decision
            And that these were my final days.

The most beautiful moment of the Selma/Montgomery
Journey was that while standing in a driving
Rain storm petitioning for the right
To demonstrate, the crowd
Kept thinning out to there were only a few
Standing soaked in the rain. I kept
Moving up and all at once I
Realized I was in the front of the line, shoulder
To shoulder with the Good Doctor, Martin
Luther king, Jr. I am warmed
By his spirit to this day, and never forget I
Was blessed on my Journey here to
Stand side by side with one of most illustrious and courageous
Heroes of the twentieth century.
I returned home to Pittsburgh from Montgomery,
Graduated from Duquesne, signed up for
The Peace Corps, but decided on the
War on Poverty instead.
I became a Neighborhood Youth worker and co-director
Of a tutorial/recreational center. It was the Poverty
Program at its finest and the Wall Street Journal wrote

That Pittsburgh was one of the best cities in
    America for proper use of the war on poverty
        Funds.
            It was a joy to work with the
Children in the after school programs. There was
        Remedial and tutorial help from grades 1–12,
By professional part time educators and great volunteers
        From the local high schools, like St. Raphael's
            In neighboring Morningside.
It was an inspiring program that like Head Start should still
    Be available for children today. RFK, Jr., said in
        1968 that 1.5 billion dollars in funds would
    Only be the start, and that over a few years it certainly
        Would take 20 billion dollars annually.
If it takes star dust to create a star, then my
Involvement with the children was truly star dust and
    I was mesmerized by their charm. I helped the
        Boys who got in trouble, by going to court
            With them and promising the Judge
    They would have a community representative keeping
        Tabs on them. I took my Saturdays with a

Friend and we collected furniture from wealthier
>Families and transported to the
>>Homes in our neighborhood surrounding
>The center. I rented the truck, bought the cigars and
>>Considered it my weekend fun activity.

I always sang with the children especially if an instructor
>Was late or had to be absent that day from the program.
>>In singing with the children I discovered that

Four of them just lit up the room. They were Arlette Price,
>Denise Peays, Yvonne Tucker and Dolly Lisa Elliot.

We started singing together and called ourselves,
>>"Don and the Pennies". They were only eight
>And nine years old and their parents entrusted them to
>>My care for rehearsals and singing engagements.
>>>I was their "Mister Don" and they were the
>>Joy of my life. (See picture 1967 & 1995)

We met 25 years later and they shared with me just how
Happy they had been during those couple of years we shared.
>>We however, did not located Denise, but we
Are still looking forward to locating her someday. (See picture)
>>I returned to doing community theatre and it was with the
>Role of "Ko-Ko" in the "Mikado" that I decided I

Loved the roar of the grease paint and the smell
 Of the crowd. I had thought about Child Guidance
  And Law School, but chose going on to
   Mountain Playhouse, Jennerstown, Pa.,
And then to New York
I have to thank a wonderful woman, Margaret McFarland,
 Of the Arsenal Guidance Center in Pittsburgh. I
  Had the "Pennies" perform for the center one
Day and we talked after the show. I told her I was
Confused about career and she said, "Follow your creative urges
 First, it will bring much to any career you later decide
  Upon." She had known Erik Erickson, a great
   Child psychologist, and she mentioned
That it was so important to his career that he was firstly,
 An artist.
There are moments when we penetrate the where to go part
 Of this Journey. It's an opening up of our hearts
  And minds when we finally feel we have
   Found the Path we should follow.
    This was my moment.

CHAPTER 10: P.A.T.H.

There is a path I was on to Success and there was a Path
    That I was trying to find that was leading me to Paradise.
Success is the sweet reward of this life, and Psalm 1,
    Lets us sing daily that creation's wish is that
        "Success will attend all you do." The Path to
            Paradise on the other hand, is the one
    That we journey with confidence that we have to love this
        World, even though we may not be of this World.
Walt Whitman walked the streets of Brooklyn and Manhattan
    And he found a way to transcend this world. His poetry
        Is so uplifting.
Easy to follow and sometimes hard to understand,
    He was a man whose every
        Breath was a Prayer of Poetry.
He has been described as one of those
    Extraordinary individuals who
        Live on this earth and who possess a
            Cosmic Consciousness.
I did a play for the 1976 Centennial and played Walt Whitman.
    I felt a kinship with this creative soul, who not only

Wrote some of the world's finest poetry, but
> Who found time to become a
>> Nurse and tend to the needs of the
>>> Men who had been ravaged by the
>> Civil War.

Walt had found a path to paradise. I wanted a Path, but
> Wasn't quite sure where to begin.

Then while visiting the A.R.E. bookstore in Virginia Beach,
> I discovered some writings of the prophet, Edgar Caycee.

In his journal he lists the most important things to do for the day
> And one of those important items was to have eight glasses
>> Of water daily. Such a simple act, but he wanted
>>> To be sure he did not forget to do it every
>> Single day.

I was inspired, so I began to write down what I wanted to
> Do each day, and the most important things I
>> Wanted to do each day.
> They included praying, to meditate the Psalms,
>> To run, and to read. As I concentrated on

Those few things I began to realize I wanted to include
> Others in my day and to re-call them to my

Mind. It developed over the years until my four

Simple habits daily were now 16. I had four

Groups of four and I created an acronym

For each of the four and they became

My *P.A. T. H.*

Path One (P.A. T. H. I)

P—Prayer, Praying the Psalms

   A—Affirm who I am

      T—To Re-call everyone I have ever known

         H—Hear the Voice for God in everything

Path Two (P.A. T.H. II)

P—Praise the Heavens with Song & Smiles

   A—A letter or a call to a friend, remember birthdays, anniversaries

      T—To Run and To Read, for mind and body

         H—honoring the body with Health, Exercise, Care

Path Three (P.A. T. H. III)

P—Power and the realization of a relationship with a Creator

   A—Abundance, sharing the daily bread of prosperity

      T—To Thank, the heavens, the earth, my family

         H—Holiness and the ability to share Happiness

Path Four (P.A.T.H. IV)

P—Peace, Peace in the World, Peace at Last
    A—A Course in Miracles, lessons for daily happiness
        T—To forgive, and to forgive 7 times 70
            H—Heal myself, others, the world
      These paths led to great rewards and riches
Of the Spirit that included gentleness, tolerance,
      Patience, love and joy. It enabled me to
    Heal those I cared for, friends and family alike
      When they were in depression, despair,
        Sickness and sorrow.
I could sense the power of the Universe; I could hear the voice for
    God, I could forgive, as a Son of God should, I began to
      Penetrate the mystery, I could expect Miracles,
        I became a Breath of Understanding and
Felt the sheer ecstasy of being a co-creator, I could see light every
    Where, I began to create Star Dust.

CHAPTER 11: 1968

It was still going to be many years on the path to success
    And following the career path, before I would be
        Able to follow that P.A.T. H. that is leading
            To the stars.
    I was 28 years old now and
I cared only about the path to becoming a star in the theatre.
    I had given up on a belief in God,
        In prayer, and of course
    Given up on our country.
I now feared that the society
    That would assassinate Martin, John and
        Robert, just like it had
    Abraham, would kill me for Loving justice and peace.
    Marianne Williamson, author of
        "Healing of America", and one of my
Favorite people on this earth, said in a talk she gave in
    Ft Lauderdale, that after the deaths of our heroes
        We were afraid to get involved
Because we might get killed, but today society
    Would have to accept that we must be

Involved and that we no longer feared death.
I drifted out on a sea of fear, rather than to continue
    To help end racism and hate. If Malcolm, John
        Robert and Martin could not improve
    This world what did it need with a Gump like me.
So the path was to head through the Mountains of
    Pennsylvania and Summer Stock, and on to New
    New York to become an Actor.
I kissed my little Singing Pennies good-bye,
    Tore up the application to
        Notre Dame Law School,
        Gave away all
    My furniture and headed back into
        The very forests I had come from
When I was a deer searching for the streams.
    I had forgot, I had forgot to remember why
    I had wanted to be a child of God.
        I had forgot to Remember and
        Now I was alone again
        In the woods.

CHAPTER 12: GOODNIGHT LASSIE, GOODNIGHT MOM

I want to take you back to Pittsburgh and all
That led up to the summer of 1968. A summer
Of Mystery, Sorrow and above all
The summer of my Epiphany.
I grew up in the town of Lawrenceville in Pittsburgh, Pa along
Allegheny River, and the birth place of Stephen
Foster, American songwriter. I sang the
Songs of Foster for my father from age 5 years old till
About 11 years old. I loved those songs and
It was to turn out that over a half century
Later I would find Fosters music
At the center of my life once again, as I became a
Director of an annual Concert for peace in
Florida on the Swanne River
At the Stephen Foster Memorial Park.
The copy of the concert program and poetry is in
Appendix D—Peace at last Concert.
I attended the Dome Movie Theater on Butler Street, a half block
From my home. It was 13 cents for a double feature, serial and
Cartoon. At night the cost was increased to 16 cents,
But then they added the News. Kent's Candy

Store was next door and for the remaining 12 cents out
    Of the Quarter movie money, you could get about
        Two dozen pieces of candy dropped into
            A small brown bag called a penny bag.
One of the earliest films I remember was the original "Lassie".
    I returned to my home following the film feeling
        A craving for the brand of warmth pictured.
My stepmother, Mary, was a very caring person of the five
    Of us, but she never went much for hugs and kisses.
Lassie got a lot of hugs, and if I was not going to get them
    Then I knew I if I ever became a father, I would hug
        My children. My childhood prayer was a vow
    That as a parent I would always try to offer a special
        Closeness into the family circle.
This call to fatherhood included a spiritual vocation that
    Maybe I should be a priest and then a father to many.
I always listened intently and seemed to be able to hear
    What was being said between the lines, and I
        Always was to offer in my own simple way
            Some kind words. It was the beginning
Of developing the "friendship therapy" that I was to share

With many wonderful people over the years. I had
    Returned from the Navy at twenty-one years
        Old so as a freshman at Duquesne University
I was just a little older and wiser. Despite a
    Grueling schedule of a six night work week,
        And studies, I always found time for
           Those in need of sharing some
Problem. I was to become inspired by the works of Adler,
    Jung, Freud, Erik Erickson, Rollo May and Carl Rogers,
        Despite the fact I was a Philosophy/Theology
        Student, I immersed myself in their writings that
Would give me a better understanding of friends
    Who need to share their most secret thoughts
        And problems. I was at the University
When Adrian Van Kaam, published a review of "Existential
    Psychology." I was enjoying my own studies of the
        Philosophers from the Greeks to the Existentialists,
And was most influenced by Gabriel Marcel and Martin
    Heidegger. My favorite genius was a
Paleontologist by the name of Pierre Teilhard de
    Chardin, author of "The Phenomenon of Man."

Inspiration mostly came from such wonderful books as,
The Brothers Karamazov, Zorba the Greek, Don Quixote,
The Lord of the Rings, The Merlin Trilogy,
The Works of Shakespeare, Moby Dick and then in 1982,
Winters Tale.
Thank you William, Fyodor Dostoyevsky, Nikos Kazenjatkis,
Cervantes, Mary Stewart, Herman Melville and
Mark Helprin for making
Life so grand. My choice, for book
Of the century was certainly,
"Winters Tale", by Mark Helprin. I am part
Irish and appreciate James Joyce, getting
Vote for "Ulysses", but read Mark and
Judge for yourself.
So listening to people became my favorite hobby. I was
Always ready to make myself available. My
Own technique for this "Friendship Therapy"
Was what I called the six-hour session.
It was just an evening of conversation over coffee or a
Cognac or glass of wine.
I discovered that if

You really allow someone to share his or her problems in trust,
And share a little about yourself, the take your own
Tee-shirt off strategy, they relax, unwind and
Generally say what they really think
Is the problem.
It was always interesting that at the moment they
Have an awakening, a glaze goes over their eyes,
And they are no longer listening. They are
Smiling because they are hearing that
They just voiced what the heck the problem is and
What they should do about it, and they are
Anxious to get moving, saying
Goodnight Don, and
Get on with their lives. Amen.
Ah, healing is truly in our own friendship therapy, our own
Friendly relationship with one another, and in our
Ability to Listen and in their ability to
Hear the Voice of their Self.
I had such a moment in 1962 with my dear parents, Daniel and
Mary. They were contemplating a separation after
Seventeen years in this their second marriage.

They could not even speak to one another. I sat at
    The kitchen table in our home in Morningside and
        Planted myself like a tree in Lebanon.
           I listened, they screamed,
I listened, they walked out of the room on one another,
    I listened, she cried,
        I listened, he stuttered, and
    I could feel the intensity of the insults and
        Humiliation they were able to
           Volley at each other.
All of a sudden, Mary turned on me and said,
    "You children never loved me either,"
Whoa! Where did that come from?
    In my surprised silence, tears came and
        Thoughts harbored back to the
Lassie fantasies and all those hugs I had always missed.
    I always tried to please her and win her love,
        And my sister Mary, said later that
           Out of the four, I was her favorite.
She would worry and get upset at things I did more than
    The others, but I had never knew that.

"That's not true" she said, "it's just that I did not give
>   Birth to you and it's been hard to love you like you
>   Were my very own." We wept together,
>   And my father just sat there stunned
>   At us crying together. I hugged
>   Them both that night. They made up and attended
>   Church together and lived
>   The next few years in peace.
They both died within seven years of that
>   Experience, she of cancer and he of a broken
Heart. His words at her funeral were,
>   "Well it's time for me to go."
>   "Come Dad", I said, "you'll be okay."
Six months later he died of…pneumonia.
>   How did he know? He knew.
I am his son and I understand, for I know to the day,
>   How long I am going to be here to try and
>   Bring peace and joy to those around me.
>   I have penetrated one Mystery for sure, and that is the
>   Mystery of when. I have no fear of death,
>   And continue to defy it by
Creating daily a little star dust to prepare for my Journey.

Returning to that summer of '68 that was filled with
Sorrow and of mystery, it was also filled with
Discovery and ecstasy and the
Revelation of my transformation from
A deer of the forest to
A dear person.
In the mountains of Pennsylvania, where I had roamed as a deer,
And very near where I was conceived, I stayed at an Inn
One night after the theatre. I was with a very special
Love and never forgot her mystical hold
On me. The night it was stranger
Than ever for it was dark in the room, and I could not
Even see her. This at the moment I was as
Old as my mother had been when she conceived me, and
Only a few miles away in those very mountains
Where I had been conceived.
Now in a trance of pleasure and joy, more
Happy than I had ever been in my life till then, I
Felt as though there were no walls to the room,
Or roof to the Inn. That I was as part of
Nature as much at the trees that I could

Now see swaying as two deer that just stood
    Like silent spectators to this romantic interlude.
My birth mother, Mildred once spoke to me about what
    She considered the happiest moment of her life
        And it was that June of "39 in the
            Mountains of Pennsylvania when
                She became pregnant with
                    Me.
In the Quiet of my Mind that night
    It became very clear I was the deer
        That had watched two people
    Laughing and dancing and a
Thought in the mind of God became flesh.
A few weeks later riding down the same mountain side
    Two deer walked out in front of the car in
        Broad daylight. I pulled the car
            Over and got out and stood there
                Not moving a muscle. We
Starred at each other for the longest time, and then
    They ran into the woods. It was still to take

Another quarter of a century of searching the streams,
Climbing the mountains of myself, uniting
In Love, and having my own children,
To realize that I had made the
Right choice to come out of the woods, and
Into the heart of Happiness.
As the summer of '68 went on, I was devastated by losing
What I thought for sure was the love of my life.
I held a letter in my hand that simply
Said, "it's over." I had been
Writing with joy everyday to someone visiting overseas and
With no knowledge it was over. I cried.
I awoke the mornings following and started to run the
Quiet roads. I ran by a house one morning and
Noticed that in front of house there was a collie lying in front
Of its doghouse. Over the next few mornings, it
Crept closer to the side of the road, till one morning
It just stood there waiting for me.
"Hey, Lassie, want to go for a run?", and
did she ever. We ran for miles and
I always returned her to her owner's home, and she would
Obediently walk down to her doghouse. I would

Always wave goodbye and never took her to my
    Little cottage I was living in near the theatre.
One afternoon I received word that my mother, Mary
    Had died. In our family we never said stepmother.
        We had two mothers and Mary was as much
            My mother as Mildred was.
I was to finish the performance that night, and then
    Leave the next morning for Pittsburgh.
In the middle of the play I looked at the actress across from
    Me and forgot the lines. I couldn't even remember
        The play I was in. I was stunned by grief
        And my soul was mute, and now
            So was the actor.
She was a wonderful actress, Nan Wilson was her
    Name and she took each one of my lines and
        Turned them into a question. All I
Had to do was give her a yes or a no, and for awhile
    I could just manage to shake my head in
        Agreement or disagreement. She
Helped me through my agony, and after a few minutes,
    The actor in me returned and I was able to complete the

Play and bow for the curtain call. I slowly took off my
    Make up and looked in the mirrors. All I could
        See was myself in every mirror. I was surrounded
        By me.
The cast wished me a good night, and two dear
    Actors Dennis & Jo Cunningham gave me
        Comforting hugs. I was left there
Alone and it hit me again. Mary was gone,
    My second mother was gone. I prayed aloud,
    "Oh please, I just can't be alone tonight."
However, I knew it had to be and I left the theatre alone.
I walked out into the starry night.
    All of a sudden something was moving
        Very quickly towards me and I
        Became frightened as I lifted my hands
        Up to my face to protect myself.
She, my running partner, my beautiful collie, jumped on
    Me and was crying and panting and making a
        Fuss the way happy dogs do when they
        Make a big doggie deal over you.
I was amazed, I was petting her and talking to her, and asking,

"How did you know? How did you find me?"
She had never been to my cottage after our runs,
And never to the theatre down the road.
How good it was to walk into
The night now with my friend telling her, "I am taking you
Home." I never met her masters, I never
Knew her name, and now I was walking down a
Star lit mountain road, laughing, healing, and
Even singing to her aloud, as I sometimes
Did on our morning runs.
"This is it good pup," I said, figuring she would
Go to her doghouse. As I looked back
I noticed she was doing something she had never done,
And that was she was following me. "Oh no
You don't," I chastised her, and took her all the way back
Down the yard to her doghouse. I had to repeat this
Several times. Finally, I inched away slowly and I
Could see she was going to behave as she laid her head on
Her paws. I kept turning around for a while to make
Sure I was not being followed then broke
Into a run all the way back to my cottage.

I sat down so refreshed by the night's run and all of the
Activity musing the passing of Mary and
The strange instincts of a dog. She certainly had
Come to rescue my saddened heart.
I started to cry wishing my love of the mountains were
There with me when I heard
A dog outside my door. It was not barking, it was crying,
And it was a whimpering beautiful sound that
Led me to open the door and let her into
My room. I hugged her, and
Realized she must have still followed me, because she
Had never been here till this night.
I watched what she did next with even more surprise.
She laid down beside my bed, and then
Simply went off to sleep.
I laughed as I went off to bed. I knew I was going to sleep
Very peacefully.
As the rhythm of her breathing started to
Lull me off, I was fully aware of the miracle.
I had cried out and I was answered: I was not alone tonight.

I believe my dear second mother,

    Mary,

  Looking down from

    Her star that night, got a big kick

Out of seeing the two of us.

    I had longed for closeness,

      And now that she was

  Gone I truly felt her love.

I can remember my last few words,

    Before I was peacefully bedded

      Down by Universal Powers,

        "Goodnight Lassie,

          Goodnight Mom."

CHAPTER 13: THE YEARS 1969–1974

Dad died. He said he would not be here long after Mary's
Death and how right he was. He was a wonderful
Irishman, a great policeman, a proud father,
And a little too proud to bear my
Lovely and zany mother, Mildred.
I think of him often and talk to him to this day under
The stars, as I do my beautiful sister, Mickey,
But that's a few years away yet.
Dad had two words he used over and over with me,
As I grew up, and they were, "Be yourself".
He especially said this if I was boasting
Or just so happy I had taken a
First place in a cross-country
Meet. I was sad that he didn't simply say
"Way to go son," but it always hit me
That maybe he wanted me to remain modest no
Matter what the achievements.
I graduated from the American Musical & Dramatic Academy in
New York, studying with Richard's father, Philip Burton,
And the marvelous present director of the Academy, David Martin.

While at the academy I was alone for awhile, but
I met a beautiful woman who I lived
With for a few years. I had never
Liked being alone and I always dated
The loveliest of women. In Italy it had been Teresa
Tutino, from Positano, and back in Pittsburgh,
It was Mitzie, Nancy, Candy, Sharon,
Kathy, Dorothy and Joanne.
Now in New York I was to be always safe and always
Protected by a woman's love, and Mary, Barbara,
Cheryl and Donna brought such joy. I was
Never to be alone again after that
Night in the mountains when second mother, Mary
Smiled down on Lassie and me. To all the
Women that I have loved, you don't know this but
Each day I recall you to my thoughts, and
Send forth a prayer that you are especially blessed,
I have never forgotten you and I never will.
I started out doing off-off Broadway, a way to showcase
Your talent. I became an extra on soaps and in films
And kept up my voice and acting lessons.
I was cast in my first soap opera, by a

Wonderful casting director by the name of Susan Slade. She was also the author of The play, "Ready When You Are C. B." I was in an audition for CBS TV with a group of casting directors from Various shows like "Love of Life" "Love is a Many Splendored Thing" and "Where the Heart Is". Karen De Vito and I did a scene from "Luv" and five Minutes later when we finished, the directors Were still leaning their chins on their Hands showing no excitement or interest. Susan jumps right Up out of her chair and shouts so loud they all bolted Upright, "Wow, that was terrific." Thanks Susan, How my heart was broken when I came back in 1971 from Lock Haven, Pennsylvania and a Summer Stock job, To find out you had passed away at a young age. My biggest fan and up till that moment, a woman who once Whispered to me on the set, "You won't be an extra Forever." Had she lived, I believe she would have taken care of That, but without her, I was always an extra and bit for the Soaps, including "The Doctors."

Next came my off-Broadway debut in a revival of

"The Madwoman of Chaillot". It was directed
By Robert Henderson and one extraordinary
Cast including Blanche Yurka, who had acted as Madame Lafarge
In "Tale of Two Cities" and had to be carried into the
Theatre each night she was now so old. Jacqueline
Susann who had published a blockbuster, "Valley of the
Dolls", and others of fame. However, the
Star for me was Peggy Wood, who had played on the wonderful
TV show, "I remember Mama". I had a rocking chair
That was children's size and I rocked in it from
"The Lone Ranger" in 1948 till "I Remember Mama in the 50's.
"American Bandstand", "Gun Smoke" and "Have Gun
Will Travel" were the end of watching TV unless it
Was the Academy Awards, the Olympics or Watergate
Investigations.
I was on the same stage as Peggy Wood, Mama,
To a kid in a rocking chair, and I was
Also able to hold her hand and
Gaze into those beautiful eyes, and tell her of the
Joy I had experienced watching her as I
Was growing up in Pittsburgh.

I had worked as a host at the incredible Four Seasons Restaurant
On Park Avenue since I had arrived in New York, and
Met the executive secretary, Margaret Stephenson,
Who was to become a friend for the next
Thirty years and never missing a year with the most
Incredible Chinese New Year's card that she designed
So beautifully. Jacqueline Susaan came
Into dine with her husband one night after our little
Off-Broadway played closed. She dined in
Elegance and walking out she stopped me and said,
"Don't worry about all this, you'll be back
On stage soon, I know it." She died a
Few years later, but she got her wish for a little gift
That she could at least write before she died.
There was going to be another actress
Come into my life that also prayed that she could just
Have a little time to write before she left this earth. Her name
Was Deborah Howe. Her husband, Jim Howe directed
Us in some comic off-off Broadway plays and
Reader's Theater and they were just a funny
Delightful couple. One day walking around New York, I asked
Her if she was happy. She said that being married to Jim

And acting made her the happiest woman in the
>World. This was just a few years before
>>Cancer was going to take her away,
>But I'll return to her wonderful story in
>>A short while.

I began regular waitering to make a little more
>Money than hosting and went from the
>>Copacabana to Maxwell's Plum

To Broadway Bay and Bay 100 and finally to
>Sardi's over the next 10 years. My favorite

Night working at the Copa was posing for a picture with
>Friends who came to see the star singing
>>That evening. It was Tony Bennett

And he brought down the house. He was so gracious.
>I treasure the picture and the memory.

I lived in the Village for awhile and one rainy day in
>New York I was on a subway. Across from me
>>Sat Al Pacino leaning on his umbrella, and

Just gazing out the window, so lost he jumped up after the
>Subway passed his stop. I didn't bother him with
>>Saying things like "man, your performance in "Does

A Tiger Wear a Necktie" so inspired me that I use your

Monologue from the play for all my auditions." No, I
    Just watched him and thought to myself, he looks
        Like he just closed a deal on a play or something
That probably was mind blowing. Not long after "The Godfather"
    Opened to audiences that still to this day vote it the number
        One film of all time, or at least close to that.
I wanted to ask him, would you take me to a film with you, I'd
    Take the job of your stand-in while you sat in the
        Winnebago preparing for your next scene. I
Didn't ask him. But I did end up working as an extra in two
    Films he did, "Godfather Two" and "Dog Day Afternoon".
        I kept studying and working long nights,
And missed a spiritual relationship. I had forgotten my God,
    I even denied Him. Thanks to a woman, Gale
        Weiss, I started chanting and practicing Buddhism,
        Nichiren Daishonin sect, and chanting, "Nam
"Nam Myoho Renge Kyo", It was a great practice and thank
    You Barbara and Mary for sharing it with me. It was to
Prepare me for once again finding my way back to Christian
    Spirituality and sharing the Episcopal Church with Cheryl.
        (See Appendix B—Peacocks on the Snow)

With my dear brother, Jesus, I began to remember
    Once again who I was. I wanted to help
Again and I chose to become a drama teacher in a drug
    Rehabilitation program thanks to Fred Labelle,
Who had remembered me from Pittsburgh and my work with
    The children. I loved the work. I went to New York
        University for a Therapeutic Recreation Workshop with the
        Renowned Edith Ball of the
    Recreation field and she talked me into
Accepting a fellowship to work on my Master's Degree.
    I could have gone on the road with Ingrid Bergman in
    "Captain Brassbound's Conversion", but accepted the
    Chance to go back for more education. I worked
Under one of the most incredible people now living, and that
    Is Stephen Chinlund, presently the director of the
    Episcopal Aid Society. I was promoted over and
Over till I became Recreation Supervisor for the State of
    New York Narcotics Commission. Working with
Female heroin addicts at the Manhattan Rehabilitation Center,
    At 42nd street and 10th avenue became a joy and I
    Almost decided to leave acting and work
    With addicts as a career, but once

Again I heard the sirens of the theatre call
And I was off to North Carolina to
Perform again in one of my
Favorite plays, "Teahouse of the August Moon".
I was so happy to have worked so
Closely with those who needed help.
I was also so happy that I once again I was
Remembering why I had left the peace of the
Forest for this terribly noisy and competitive world.
I lifted my eyes to the heavens nightly once again
And walked the forests and the ocean sides
With a prayer in my heart. It repeated
Over and over;
I remember, I remember.
Thank you O starry heavens for reminding me who I am,
I remember, I remember
Where I am going.
I was back on a Path again and although I prayed
I would never forget again, of course, I
Was to forget, but for now I was
As happy as Zorba dancing under the Stars.

CHAPTER 14: FORGET ABOUT IT

Remember who you are. The words are always softly
Reminding me of my Journey and why I choose to
Be here. I loved playing in "The Fantasticks",
The longest running musical in the world.
It's a treat for every parent to take their children to this
Endearing show at a lovely off-Broadway
Theatre in the Village. I sang it's
Most popular song, "Try to Remember" and like
Madonna's haunting "Remember" I always
Feel like I am chanting or hearing spiritual sonnets. Hamlet's
Father comes to him as a ghost and pleads, "Remember
Me" and Simba the lion cub looks up to the star of Musafa
Burning brightly and is reminded to "Remember who you are".
I look up at the stars and my father still
Reminds me "Remember my words,
Be yourself". In being myself, I was in love with
Becoming an actor. All the World was a Stage, and
I was merely a player, but Shakespeare
And the playwrights let me be myself. Each play was
An incredible Journey and always a reminder.

Each novel was a reminder. I danced with
    Zorba the Greek, and threw myself on the
Ground to kiss the earth like Aloysha Karamazov. I returned
    To the Psalms and David once again sang to me
    Of right conduct and not acting in brutish ways. In the
    Song of Songs, Solomon spoke of how
Beautiful it was to be smitten by Love, and glance from
    My Love gave the sweet desire for the
Unity that comes from the creator and
    His creation. At times I actually thought I
Was remembering Eternity. I heard ancient melodies and songs
    That touched my soul of Memory and the Music played
    Over and over as my Spirit listened to its lyrics.
Remember who you are,
    Remember why you have come here,
    Remember what your function is,
    Remember where you are going.
As I remembered I began to realize that the
That I was discovering what was really important. What
    Action could I do now, Living in the Now and
    Forgetting the past and not worrying about the Future?

In forgetting the past and especially forgiving
    Myself my own mistakes, I pierced another
        Part of the Mystery. It was to
            Un-do.
Un-do the past, the pain, the problems, the
    Prejudices, the petty gripes, the
        Poisonous thoughts, the
            Prison of my own will that was
Preventing me from attaining the prize of
    Happiness.
        Like the hero in "Braveheart" I sighed,
"Love ya, always have." My Creator sent the same
    Message, "Love ya, always have." As a
        Messenger I am asked to continue to
Pass on this lesson of peace until the world
    Remembers
        That Peace is the only state we should
            Be living in together.
    Everyday I experience someone saying
        That they will not forget or forgive. They have
Been insulted, angered, betrayed, made light of,

Abused, mis-used, battered and even injured.
  They are sometimes part of the same family,
In any case they no longer smile at one another
  Or forgive the affront, insult or badly spoken
    Words. In essence that it is difficult to
  Forgive another's mistake when they should be
Recognizing that we are all Divine.
I have been injured in spirit and my
  Feelings have been hurt but I have
    Learned three words which have
Become for me the best stress release I could have
  Found. They are "forget about it".
I laughed when in the movie "Donnie Brasco"
  Al Pacino, Johnny Depp and cast
    Have a lot of fun with the
      Expression, "forget about it".
  It's more than an expression; it's also a mantra
    Or a prayer. It's a gift from the angels
      Who hover over me to get my
Attention to smile and not be so
  Concerned with worldly peccadilloes.

I have learned with embracing
> Psalm 91 that I have no fear of the

Outrageous slaughter that may be going on to
> My right and to my left.

The angels are protecting me and will not allow me to
> Dash my foot against the stones.

I believe that is true and when I do trip
> I have this great ability to have that split
>> Second ability to re-call "I will not fall"
>
> And I do not.

I now look at the world that I live in and forget
> About falling and I start to remember,
>
> I walk in light. I begin to walk
>
> Out of darkness, sadness, sickness, accidents,

Remembering that I am a Son of God.
I truly have begun to realize that I am holy and that
> There is nothing my holiness cannot do.

One thing I feel for sure.
> I do not have to accept this insane world.
>
> "Forget about it."

My desire is now to un-do the mistakes and to

Forgive and forget. I want to remember what the
    Earth is like when I enter the space of the
Angels. I have discovered in the stars and
    In the universe my own divinity.
I now face my biggest challenge of this lofty
    Living and with Pascal treat the little things
        As though they were great, and the
Great things as though they were little.
    It is interesting is that little things
Irk me the most and keep me truly forgetful about the
    Great and the beautiful life I have chosen.
I continue a Journey and my ascent to the heavens and
    I certainly do not have time for road rage,
Frustration in ticket lines, and reacting to all those
    Seemingly irksome habits that folks do as they
        Cross my path. I have begun to smile
At the victory over being irked by petty conduct.
    My car is a sanctuary. It's a place to be alone,
        To sing, to meditate, to create and to
Practice how to "forget about it".

I have great blood pressure and great health, and
    I have become holier as well as healthier
        As I grow in love and light. Sometimes
I have an episode of light and those are moments I
    Know for sure I am creating star dust.
I am walking in a Forest of Stars, I want to change
    A mean-spirited world into a happier place
        Where there is Peace at Last.
I want to begin to truly desire the
    Good, the true, and, the beautiful.
I have begun and I began it by Remembering,
    Remembering who I am.
        You have
    My prayer and
        My daily re-call for your
            Blessings.
Remember, my dear friend,
    Remember who you are.

CHAPTER 15: THE YEARS 1975–1978

Broadway! I made it!
I am standing on stage and they are reading the Clive Barnes review.
He is the New York Times Theatre critic and he
Saw the show in preview.
He loves the show he praises me as the
"Psalm Singing Padre".
Tears fill my eyes.
A friend, Anne Tarpey, who attended my
Debut, that beautiful March Sunday in 1975,
Said, "I could go home now." Anne along with
Charles Craig, Charlie Stavola, Tina Kaplan, all graduates of
AMDA, were on my side. Also were my dear friends,
Jim and Deborah Howe, and Cheryl Horne.
The show was "The Lieutenant", and it nominated for
Four Tony awards including Best Musical 1975.
Along with "Shenandoah" we lost to "The Wiz". "The Lieutenant" was a
Rock-opera about the My Lai massacre.
The war in Vietnam was still fresh in everyone's mind so it was a hard
Show to enjoy. Bill Martin, the director, had
Taken it from an off-off Broadway showcase
To Broadway. Chorus Line was to take the same route and

Be very successful. We closed in nine performances.
Our show should have hidden
Out off-Broadway in the Village for a few
Years and I am certain that it could still be running
Today. Historically as well as dramatically,
It was a brilliant show.
I went on to Boston to do a musical called "Love me, Love
My Children." It was nice in that my old friend from
High school, college and the Navy was there
With his wife, so I was re-united with
Bob & Flo Limpert.
In Boston I met a dear woman from a Public TV show,
Evvy Titleman, who introduced me to the
Boston Marathon and it excited me
Enough to get back to running. I made it to Boston
For the Marathon four years later. Evvy and
Her husband David were to become
Great friends and she definitely proves that
We never stop finding new friends,
Who encourage and inspire us on this Journey.
The bicentennial was incredible.

I went out to meet the Tall Ships that sailed
Into New York from all over the world to celebrate our
200 hundredth year. Queen Elizabeth rode up
Park Avenue and Jimmy Carter came in
To win the Democratic nomination. I was able to play
Walt Whitman in a production called
"The Wound Dresser". I was
Running down the Jersey shore on the 4th of July,
Thinking of Walt and writing poetry.
(Appendix B—Running for America)
To this day I share with Walt his feelings
For America and for being in touch
With all around us, and I use his poetry for the concert
I hold each year called "The Peace at Last Concert".
I was now taking voice lessons five days a week. Thanks to
My dear friends, Barbara Idelson, Caroline Thomas and
Her father Curtis Thomas, I was to meet
Harold Kravitt. An opera basso who
Played in the Wagner Festival in Germany in 1933,
Quite a feat for a Jewish boy from New York,
And who was to be beat out of a position

Of leading basso for the Metropolitan Opera, by
    None other than Ezio Pinza of "South Pacific"
        Fame.
I remember Harold. His gigantic voice and his
    Powerful presence. At my first visit he
        Said, "sing" and I did. "You will
Need lessons five days a week my son" he said.
    Hello Harold, I thought, I'm thinking of
        One half hour a week when you
Get done telling me your fee is going to be somewhere
    Around $50 an hour minimum. I had been
Paying by the hour for voice lessons in New York, and
    It was getting more expensive all the time.
I never got to tell him what I was thinking. "Stop thinking
    About money when I'm talking to you. I know your
        Situation. I know you waiter on tables, I know
            You struggle. You give me $5.00 for
Each daily session, is that fair?" I feel in love with
    My mentor. I was there daily and sometimes
        Those sessions were over two hours.
Thank you Harold, you were the prince. He used to walk his

Older brother up and down the apartment hallway,
During the lesson. Harold was already eighty
Years old and his brother was over 90.
(See Appendix B—Prince of the Long Journey)
I am still singing today, and I know that I will sing
Till I am ninety like Harold did because
Of the great lessons about the voice he taught me, and also because once
Again I am blessed with a great teacher, Barbara Wack
Frank Sinatra once stood at his piano and sang for
Harold with hopes of training with him. Harold
Told me he said,
"There's nothing I can teach you, you have the
Technique and the talent to sing for many, many years."
Nice prediction Harold, but also nice knowing
You and your sister Jenny, who made
Sure we had tea and discussion
In the kitchen with her husband Victor. Also,
For introducing me to your wonderful student, Bill
Thourlby, author of "Passport to Power" and other
Books and who to this day is the Prince of the
New York Athletic Club.

I am running again. I circle the six miles
    In Central Park daily and it is my
        Mecca in the noisy, competitive
            And glorious city.
I am strengthened and sustained by love and
    Again without the friends in my life,
        I could not have had the soul
Of a champion. Auditioning, waitering, training
    And now running marathons in New York,
        Boston, Pittsburgh, Virginia Beach,
            And other cities. I even run
                The 50 mile in Central
Park and know what it's like to be out there for
    Seven hours and 28 minutes non-stop.
So thank you Mary, Barbara, Donna and Cheryl
    For your friendship, love and inspiration
        And most of all taking this Knight
    Of Existence up part of the seven story
        Mountain I was continuing to climb.
        (See Appendix B—Knight of Existence)
Thank you dear friends Jack Hallett and Bruce Israel

For Laughter. I will not forget that I actually
Had to lie down in the middle of the
Sidewalk so weakened with
Laughing that I could not
Even stand.
Jack Hallett was one of the few comic actors
I ever worked with that could keep
The audience in tears of laughter
For minutes responding to
His comic antics.
He literally defined "bringing the
House down."
I love the comedies and dinner theatre gave you
The opportunity to do them. In New York,
It was a chore to convince them you
Would make a good bit, or even
A good understudy.
Thanks to Warren Crane, director and producer, I was
Able to become an understudy for "Same Time,
Next Year". The original with fellow
Pittsburgh native, Charles Grodin and the
Lovely Ellen Burystn was one of my

Favorites. To become a Broadway understudy to
This treat was a joy. It also gave me a
Chance to understudy the stars
Of the national companies.
One trip was with Barbara Rush and Tom Troupe
In Toronto. I had watched Barbara in films
For years and to be now sharing
A great production in a great city was delightful.
Now thanks to Kate Pollak and Warren
Crane once again I was chosen as
The understudy for Dick Van Dyke
In the LA production of "Same Time, Next Year" with
Carol Burnett. This production was
Sold out as soon as the tickets were
Available, and it's a shame
That this was never filmed. It was wonderful.
To be at the Huntington Hartford theatre
Every night while the laughter
Hit peaks that I am certain I may never witness ever again.

The joys continued as now thanks to that talented
Jack Hallett who had drifted into directing
Stars in productions, I was to be
Second banana to one of the
Top comic banana's of all time,
Morey Amsterdam. We played
Jacksonville's famous Alhambra Theatre and
Along with Donna Drewes and Robbie Fian,
Once again I was dizzy with the laughter
And the euphoria of the audience
Being slain by a master like Morey Amsterdam.
Acting had its joys, it's standing ovations but
Something was missing. I was
Hearing a voice and it was saying "when are
You coming home and do what you were
Always meant to do."
Whatever did that mean?
I was finally going to discover that making
Star dust was going to mean
Giving up what I loved to do
For what I knew I would love even more.

CHAPTER 16: STARDOM VERSUS FATHERHOOD

What did I love even more? Was it this crazy and
Wonderful career or was it something that
I still needed to discover?
There was a night that I walked the streets of
New York thinking about all of this.
I knew it was only a matter of time. It wouldn't
Be long now and I would hit
The right play, receive my
Tony, get my movie, receive my Oscar and then
Just coast till my lifetime achievement
Award and universal praise that would be
Accorded to me for making people smile or cry,
And just entertaining them with my every
Solid performance.
So far I wasn't netting any big credits or big bucks. Yes,
It was great to work with Christopher Lloyd in
The most creative production of a season,
The Village Voice said, for "Myth Oedipus." I
Was the horse cop in "Godfather Two", a copy across
The street from the bank with Al Pacino in "Dog
Day afternoon. Working with friends like Christina Denzinger

Cheryl Horne, Mimi Bensinger
 And of course, Jack Hallett and Christopher
  Lloyd. A very happy moment of
My career was the understudy job that allowed me to
 Work with Dick van Dyke and Carol Burnett.
One night at a dinner took all of the company to in
 Hollywood, Carol looked up from her coffee, and
  Said, "Now let's see who we can help." In
   My mind I kept hearing her saying Don, let's help Don
    Get on with his career, but she said, Kate, let's
   Help Kate. It would have been nice, but I will tell
    You a story later that Carol rewarded me more
     Than I could have ever imagined.
I walked a long time that night and I needed to stop at
 A restaurant for a drink. More than the drink I needed
  To sing a song and just receive some applause
And just feel that glow I loved to feel when
 I had been performing.
  I stopped at Mrs. J's on West 72nd
   Street not from where I was living on
    The upper West Side.

One more look at the stars not realizing that night I was
Not going to become a star as much as I was going
    To begin to make star dust.
I loved Mrs. J's. The waitresses were beautiful and like
    My dear friend Anne Tarpey they were
All Broadway hopefuls and sang like birds. Eddie
    Was on the piano and he loved to play for
    One of the customers every now and
Then especially if it was a guy just to give the girls
    A little break when they were especially busy
    With the serving. I would barely have
My Dewars and soda to my lips when I would hear the
    Music of "Come back to me" being played
Which was Eddies signal that I get up there and sing with him.
    He was so good and it was
    Like you were really the top performer for
The evening. I sang a couple of songs then back to my
    Scotch and soda. Eddie stopped by on his break
To tell me a certain gentleman in a back booth
    Wanted me to stop by his table to share a drink.

Normally the customers didn't pay me much attention.
They were there to enjoy and food and the delightful
Songs of the singing waitresses.
I found myself sharing my life with this pleasant
Elderly and distinguished gentleman. He
Said he wanted to know why I had changed my name to
McGrath. I told him it really was my name and
My father was Irish. "But your mother, was
Italian and Sicilian", he said, as I
Looked at him stupefied. "How did you get that so
Correctly," I asked. "I could tell it
From the way you sang," he said.
"I want to tell you a couple of things, why don't you walk
Me home." We left the restaurant and walked for
A while in the direction of his apartment.
He started laying out a career for me that would allow me to
Sing, rather than continue to wait on tables, audition
And have to get my thrills singing in a pub for
Free. The more he talked I realized he
Was talking from some authority on the matter. When
He described the career of a celebrity and

A very successful career. I knew I was getting a
    Little scared because I was shaking all over.
        Being Sicilian myself I can not
            Repeat what he actually
    Revealed to me. Call it omerta, or call it
        Secrecy or simply call it just having
            Enough sense to know that
This was a lot bigger than I was. I had a thousand thoughts
    Rush at me in the space of my next few minutes of
        Silence.
"I can't do that, I replied, it sounds like someone will
    Want something from me." He stopped and
        Said that this was as far as he wanted
            Me to walk. "Sure, like doing
What you like to do…sing".
    I stood in front of him, my shoulders
        Slumped and my head bowed down.
He took my face in his hands, and squeezed my
    Cheek affectionately. "O Donaldo, he
        Said, "you're a nice boy, but you're
            Never going to make it."

He then slapped my cheek and no one had
    Done that since the Bishop of Pittsburgh
        Confirmed me and gave me the
            Name I had chosen as my
New spiritual name, Anthony. I didn't even
    Know at that time that it was the name
        Of my Sicilian grandfather. I
Had come full circle as an Anthony. I felt he
    Was absolving me for wanting to be
        In show business and not pay
Whatever price I had to pay to achieve success.
    I walked away, and headed towards my
        Apartment. It was late
And few people were out. I gazed up at
    The stars and I let the tears fall
        And splash the sidewalk.
As they bounced off the cement they seemed to
    To be little flashes of light. It was my
        First moment of experiencing
            Tiny specks of star dust.
                Then, once again that

Breeze from the mountains touched my face
And like that evening when the roof
Lifted off the Inn I was in the
Midst of an Epiphany and penetrating the Mystery
Of the experience of God. It was to be
The beginning of seeing the star
Dust I was creating.
I knew my elderly friend was right. I was not going to make it in
Show business. Maybe it was because I really
Was not talented enough, or because I lacked the opportunity,
Or because I spent too much time on just earning a
Living and paying the expenses an actor pays
To try and stay in the business.
I made Broadway without his help. I bowed before
A standing ovation on an Opening Night. I had
Made people laugh and cry. I had been
Reviewed well in the New York Times, but I
Couldn't boast to the fact that I made my
Living just with my theatrical work. But, with his
Help I could sing. I always wanted to sing in some way, and
If it meant singing in a lounge till 4:00 am

Maybe that would be enough reason to accept his offer.
All of a sudden I pierced another Mystery.
I realized what kind of tears were falling
From my eyes. They were tears of joy.
I understood clearly now what I wanted and
Exactly what it was I was not willing to give up to
Attain the prize. I was walking on a mist of
Understanding, and the city that I loved wrapped its
Night-ness around me with a cloak of wisdom.
I began to hear applause and I looked up into the
Starry sky. My eternal siblings were all
With me and I could sense their
Standing ovation was assuring me that this truly
One of my life's most important discoveries.
That I was to
Become what
I had always been destined to become.
That night I heard a beautiful voice and
The Mystery revealed to me by my
Father,
"You are my beloved Son in whom I take delight,

Now go and delight in the
>Career you have been
Preparing for ever since you
>Prayed as a child.
Do you remember?"
>I did remember.
>I had never forgotten that
>>Boyhood prayer.

"Let me always love a beautiful woman,
>*Let me be a good father, and above all,*
>*Let me be close to them and*
>>*Make them happy."*

CHAPTER 17: THE YEARS 1978–1979

<u>I am running along the ocean at Jacksonville</u>
And thinking about that night in New York.
I have still managed to keep working as
As actor, and thanks to my friend,
Jack Hallett, I am doing a comedy with none other
Than Morey Amsterdam. I have become a
Great runner for my age and I
Love competing in the races.
I can't seem to find the right woman and at times
I am guilty of pushing the relationships or
Making mistakes. One gentle heart
Has reminded me of my promise to never
Act in brutish ways, and to
Always choose understanding and kindness over anger.
But, I am alone again,
And I wake with a constant line from the book of
Tobit, Chapter 8, verse 8,
"It is not good for man to be alone."
I am back to New York and not concerned about myself.
A dear friend and fellow actress, Deborah Howe, is in the hospital

At St. Vincent's on 13th Street in the Village.
I visit her and laugh with her and tell her I want to act
With her again. She explains she may never be able
To walk again, but she will write
Children's' books and she will be happy.
She did write along with her husband, Jim Howe,
<u>*"Bunnicula" and "Teddy Bear's Scrapbook"*</u>.
One day at the hospital she was
Getting very tired and she whispered,
"Come close". I bent down over
Her and she raised her hand to touch my cheek,
And whispered in my ear,
"I want you to find your love."
Her arm dropped back and she fell off to sleep.
Later her husband Jim called me to
Tell me she had died. I started
Weeping on the phone. "I didn't know she was
Dying." "No, said Jim, we decided not to
Tell you. You always came and made
Her laugh."

At her memorial I was angry with Dylan Thomas,
As we cried out together in his poetry,
"Rage, Rage, against the dying of the
Light," and then I softened up
And found that W. B. Yeats, would let me
Speak of her as a hazelnut, and as the
Girl of the golden apples of the
Sun and the silver apples of the moon.
I was never to forget that night, and as her book
"Bunnicula" celebrated 20 years in
Print, I celebrated my knowing
Her and thanking her in poetry.
(See Appendix B—On the Road of Life)
I say, thank her, for I left that Memorial, and
Walked the streets of Manhattan. The
Seasons shifted into winter, and
I found myself celebrating
The Feast of Epiphany at a little church
At 46th Street and Eighth Avenue
I took a walk through the park, and
Prayed as I walked.
The Angel Raphael from the book of

Tobit was a constant companion nowadays, and
I shared my feelings of loneliness.
> ***It is not good for man to be alone."***
>> (See Appendix C—The Book of Tobit)

As I walked I also thought of Debbie and
> I asked,
>> "When is my love coming,
>>> Dear Debbie?"

Instead of heading home,
> I stopped at my favorite restaurant,
>> "The Parentheses".
>>> It was not only my favorite, but also its owner,

Jim Maceda, was a special friend and employer who always
> Took me back after I returned back to the city.

If there was a new person on the staff
> I would say hello, and let them
>> Know that I would probably be

Back working with them if I didn't get an
> Acting job within a few days.

I noticed a new waitress and walked up to
> Her to introduce myself.

"Hi, I said, I'm Don."

"Hi, she said,

I'm Debby".

I walked back to the bar and sat down.

I was sitting quietly for a moment and

I remember exactly my

Next thought,

"I just met my wife."

My prayers were answered,

Thank you Raphael.

Thank you Debbie.

CHAPTER 18: PRAYER

I am so glad you are sharing this Journey
    With me. I hope we meet and you
        Laugh with me and we sing
    And dance together across a
        Dance Floor in the
Sky lit by the stars. That is my prayer.
            Every time I pray, I join with you.
        Every time I pray
I send vibrations and ripples of tremendous caring and
        Intensity out into the Universe to touch
Those I know, those who I consciously re-call, and to
        All my new friends that I have made simply because
        I would share this Journey with you.
I seek to embrace all of mankind in the
    Circle of Eternal Love.
I desire your good favor, and ask you to pray for me.
    If we do meet let's sing, laugh and finally
        Dance together till we are exhausted
        Like Zorba the Greek teaching young Boss to
            Dance with his feet and with his heart.

So please smile and laugh during this Journey. It is a joy
To plan this Dance into Eternity.
Let us unite not in listening to the news
On radio and TV, or
The reports of violence and war. But let us
Unite in prayer so that we may hear
Each other's hearts, and if
We listen real closely, we may hear the
Voice for God.
When I hear it I am filled with Joy each moment I
Give my mind and heart to prayer.
I know that you hear an inner voice.
Some call it a Voice of God; some call it a voice of Inspiration.
Socrates called it a Daimonium, a divine inner voice, a
Kind of voice, which whenever he heard it, he always turned
Back from something he was going to do.
To me it is a voice of love and unity and it
Only requires that I take the time to Listen.
I really don't have time to give over to ideas
Of hate or the world's view on success.
The world is insane, especially when

It struggles to find a breath of fresh air. I do have
Time to love all of the creations of the
Universe that longs for caring
Inhabitants.
When it is time to Pray, I leave this insane world for
The Lawns of Heaven to find the Peace and
Quiet there and join with my brothers and sisters
That I enjoy being with. Jesus, Mary his
Mother, St. Anthony, St. Raphael, Martin Luther
King, Jr., Walt Whitman, Mother Teresa,
And Princess Di. It is my beautiful
Circle of friends that have gone before me into the
Starry night of the heavens.
Within this circle I find that I can help others,
That I can heal others, that I
Can extend a miracle to them.
Out of the twenty-four hours in a day
Nothing is more important than
The five minutes I take out of each hour to pray.
I love the Our Father and the Hail Mary even
Though I have re-written them so that

I can truly use their for communication with
My inner self, without doubting or disliking
Any of the original words.
I love the chants of the Nichiren Daishonin, and the
Buddhist tradition of really going into the
Sound to experience the mystery.
I love the Psalms of the Bible, and the spiritual
Books written by some of the prophets of our
Own time. I love taking the time to
Take good works of spirituality and use the
Most salient and wonderful points as
My prayer inspiration for the day.
I truly believe that when I pray with others that this is
The most incredible of moments, and I join with
A friend who believes in the calling for the
Friendship of one whom has gone before us. It can be
Anyone, but Jesus best describes the use of the
System by calling forth this person by
Using their name and then believing
They are truly with you. Jesus put it the very best
Way no matter who your friend is,

> *"Where two or three are gathered*
> *In my name, there I am in*
> *The midst of them."*

It is also his example to practice a great act of love,
  And a great act of forgiveness if a physical
 Act is needed, and that, is to wash the feet of another.
Love one another is the crux of prayer and
  If it is with someone you already love
    Deeply than prayer is intimate.
     It is going into the
   Inner Room, and being with that person
Till you actually lose the
    Sense of self and experience
      Oneness.
I am inspired to prayer by the Psalms, The Song of Songs,
  The New Testament, "A Course in Miracles" from
   The Foundation of Inner Peace,
"The Holy Man" by Susan Trott,
"Discover the Power Within You" by Eric Butterworth,
   "Illuminata" and "Enchanted Love",
    By Marianne Willamson,

The poetry of Maya Angelou and of Walt Whitman, the I Ching,
Tao Teh Ching , the Ancient Runes,
And most of all by the tender and spiritual
Inspiration that come from my family, friends and
Co-workers at Northwest Airlines and Hilton Banquet Dept.
I chant as I kneel before the Gohonson:

Nam Myoho Renge Kyo

(I penetrate the mystery of the
Law of cause and effect through sound) with
Nichiren Daishonin and the Buddhists
When a moment is difficult with someone
I say the prayer
Nammaskar (I salute you and your divinity)
I pray for love of all Muslims, as I pray with
Muhammad and His words from the Koran,

I send you to the while folk

And the black folk and the red folk never have I

Sent a messenger to all the folk.

I pray with Native American's Chief Seattle,

We do not weave the web of life
    We are merely a strand in it.
Whatever we do to the web,
    We do to ourselves.
I join with Unitarian Universalists,
    Agnostics and atheists in a reverent
        Choice for freedom of thought.
We acknowledge the divine
Spark within each child.
This year both Sri Chimoy and the Dalai Lama
    Have come into the twin cities. I do join in
Prayer with these great peace lovers of our
    Time for peace throughout the world.
I hope to work with Sri Chinmoy and connect the
    Bridges and rivers of the world into a flowing
        Expression of unity.
The Dalai Lama when asked by a University of Minnesota
    Student at his lecture here, "what makes you happy,"
        Responded with "Your smile is my Happiness."
    Again our very "Hi" to one another is a
Moment of prayer. To me it is the Holy Instant (Hi) to the

Dalai Lama it is Happiness Is (Hi).
>There is no greater prayer than our Hi and our
>>Smile to one another. It is the prayer of
Greeting and the wish for peace in a single word.
There was a famous Hindu Yogi, the Marareshi who taught
>Transcendental Meditation (TM). I found with a
>>Mantra I could enter into a world of bliss
>>>That allowed for peace and even the
>>>>Reduction of stress in my life.
I met another Hindu and she was a Swami. She taught me
>A prayer to Krishna called Ardas Bahee. Along with
>>Husband the Unity Minister, Jim Fisher they
Also practiced the most beautiful prayer and act of
>Forgiveness—the Washing of the Feet.
>>I washed the feet of this Swami, and she
>>>Washed mine. The electricity from
This simple act still lights and vibrates my existence many
>Years later. Go back to your beginnings, to your childhood
>>Like the Buddha, if necessary. Try to
>>>Remember what touched you at
The earliest you can re-call, and you will realize

You have a seed of something that truly wants to
>Become your Garden of Meditation and Prayer.
>>"Et introibo ad altare…I go to the altar"

I used to say all 150 Hail Mary's of the complete Rosary
>Instead of praying 150 Psalms with the monks and clerics
>>Of the church the lay people were encouraged to
>>>Pray the three mysteries of the Rosary.

There were times when I would
>Pray with my arms extended
>>Out, on my knees on

A marble altar step or cement of
>An outdoor shrine.

In the Litany to Mary the church called her the
>Star of Heaven. She was my shining star

As a young child, and I loved her. The opening
>Words spoken by the Angel Gabriel announced
>>She was to be the mother of Jesus.

The second part of the prayer I had to change for myself.

Hail Mary, full of Grace,

The Lord is with you.

Blessed are you among women,

And blessed is the fruit of thy womb, Jesus.

Holy Mary, Mother of a Son of God
Pray for us now and throughout eternity.
Amen.
I unite with my Jewish brethren and all who
    Accept the spirituality that comes from
        The Old Testament. The Psalms,
            The Song of Songs, the Proverbs,
Ecclesiastes, Ecclesiasticus, Wisdom,
                The Books of Ruth,
                    Judith, Esther,
        And especially the Book of Tobias, and
            It's beautiful explanation of prayer by
                The Angel Raphael.
                (See Appendix C—Book of Tobit)
I pray with all the prophets and love the words of Joel:
    The young men and women
    Will dream dreams.
The older men and women
Will see visions.
I was not able to understand the seeing visions part till
    I became older, but I am to share with you as
        We continue this Journey that this is

Truly a part of the path I was following.
The New Testament and the Master Teacher gave to
Me my favorite prayer. I am on the road
With Jesus, I am the Prodigal Son,
I have returned home to the Lawns of Heaven
I take my Master's hand, and I join in with
Him as we make bold to say:

Our Father, who art in Heaven,
Holy is Our Name.
Our Kingdom come, Our Will be done,
On Earth as it is in Heaven.
Give us today Joy and Abundance.
Let us share our prosperity with others,
Let us give to the world its daily bread.
Let us forgive one another.
Let us not wander into the
Temptation of making mistakes.
Let us do the right thing
Let us walk in Holiness and Grace,
Following the path of Happiness
Working Miracles and Working for Peace,

Healing and loving one another.
Then delivers us by Your Power to our Kingdom and Glory
For Thine Is the Power and the Glory and the
Kingdom Forever and Ever. Amen
      With all religions we unite in Prayer.
          With all beliefs we unite in our
              Desire for freedom.
We don't need a universal religion,
      We need an
          Universal Experience.
Perhaps the only way we will attain that
      Is in the Prayer of Silence.
In a Circle of prayer and of love and in
      Silence, I pray for
Peace at last, and that the
      Universe continue to spiral Upward into
It's Celestial Welcoming into
      Eternity.

CHAPTER 19: THE YEARS 1980–1991

Mickey died. My dear sister was with me
As I wept under the stars. She was
Still so concerned about her
Baby brother, Don, and
She wiped my tears and planted a kiss on
My soul and a promise to always be
By my side.
She was extremely happy with the
Start of my new career as husband and father.
Happiness had taken over my existence.
Debby and I were married on the Feast of
Epiphany, January 6, 1980. Her father married
Us in St. Paul at her sister and brother in law, Leslie
And Gordy's home. He made official the contract
Of marriage we had declared to each only six months after we
Had met in 1979. We were from that moment in our eyes
Married. Our ceremony was our own creation and
I included in the readings that the Feast of
Epiphany is a threefold feast that also recognizes the
Wedding feast of Cana and the Baptism of Jesus.

I began the career I had always
Desired and I can only describe
These years as the best of my life.
It was truly the beginning of the joys of
Fatherhood.
The births of my sons are still so vivid in my
Memory. If I close my eyes I can be
Back at Roosevelt Hospital and
In the beautiful birthing room, and sharing along
With our doctor, Bernardo Handzer and his
Wife and nurses. We had champagne.
We had laughter, we had tears,
We celebrated Life.
In New York we lived in the incredible
Manhattan Plaza for performing artists at
42nd Street and 9th Avenue. It was a wonderful home.
We had birthing classes with Mrs.
Elizabeth Bing at her home on 79th St.
We were her students along with
Joan Lunden whose child was born
July 4th, and our Sean, was

Born on July 6th.
It was a beautiful day and after spending hours
    In the birthing room with them. I went
        Right to our apartment, made a
"For sale" sign and went down and placed it on
    My motorcycle. I had never got hurt riding
        It but with a new son, I was not even
            Going to risk getting back on it.
Ryan came along with equal joy, as I left Sardi's that October
    Seventeenth night after a call from home.
        I was in the middle of making a
Caesar Salad at a guests table, when my
    Co-workers came over with a towel and
Wiped my hands and took over the salad making
Saying that it was time to go to the hospital for my
Wife was about to have a baby and all the customers
    Applauded as I left the floor.
    It had been the standing
    Ovation I had waited for a long time.
        Now I had two sons, Sean and Ryan,
            (See Appendix B—Our Boy, my Love)

It was wonderful being at Manhattan Plaza with
> Its subsidized rent program for performing artists
>> And support personnel. Thanks to Actors
>>> Equity, HUD, and a wonderful Episcopal
>> Minister, Rodney Kirk and Dot Slender, I was living in a great
>>> Apartment complex complete with swimming
Pool and Playground for the children.
> I now sang nightly, but it was a lullaby for putting
>> The babies to sleep. I loved playing with
>>> Them to the point of exhaustion.
> They were very energetic and playful boys. Debby
>> And I used to relax after they were off to sleep,
>>> Exhausted from the whole bath to final
>>>> Slumber exercises and ask
>> Each other, "how does a single parent do it."
> They are truly champions for it is quite the feat
>> To parent with two.
The years were joyous with baby swim at the 63rd St. YMCA,
> Programs for the kids called 1st steps, 2nds steps, pre-school,
>> Head Start, pre-K, Kindergarten, and finally into
>>> 1st grade at PS 3 in the village.

Central Park was our second home. With Sheep's Meadow,
 And a 6-mile run around the park and a double stroller
  Joined together so I could run the entire 6 Mile Loop
   With them. Yes it was just like when I
    Was young: Play, Play, Play, and
For us parents it was Fun, Fun, Fun. I created
 Rork their own Monster who they could
  Capture and silence at any time,
   And it wasn't just a claw
Like in the movie Liar, Liar, it was an authentic screaming
 Monster that could be brought to his knees
Screaming if they touched his most vulnerable point,
 His elbow.
I also became a very protective father,
 Because we had the boys in P.S. 3
In Greenwich Village. This was the school that
 Our dear Etan Patz had been abducted
  From one early morning in May
 And that is the reason we honor him
  With having the special day for
   Missing children on May 25th.

On the day he was abducted May 25, 1978. I
Realized then that the children do not have
Sanctuary. We were to move to
Minnesota in a few years and
Once again we would be reminded of this
Violation of our dear children's freedom
When Jacob Wetterling was to be
Taken from his parents and no knowledge of
What ever happened.
We did not think we would ever live in Minnesota, but
We enjoyed the Summer Vacations with Debby's
Family there. We would make a list of the
Lakes and the Playgrounds and it
Was a Paradise compared to
New York. Debby and I ran the Lakes,
And the boys enjoyed every playground we could find.
One summer our list had 24 different playgrounds
That we enjoyed.
In New York we had Clancy's Pizza across from our
Plaza home and our boys turned into Video
Game addicts, but it did not diminish that

We searched for places to play and learn. There was the
    Bronx Zoo, the Natural History Museum, and the
        Wonderful Ocean trips to Long Island.
            We vacationed in the mountains of
                Vermont and I ran the roughest
Of mountain sides and the boys rode goats and horses,
    And made friends with other New Yorkers who
        Loved to go to Maggie and Don's great
            Vermont retreats.
Debby decided that Manhattan did not offer the
    Kind of backyard that Minnesota or
Vermont had, and so in 1987 we left to start over in
    St. Paul, Minnesota.
We gave up our acting careers, which we had pretty much
    Done even with the birth of the boys, but now it
        Was official.
But these next four years became very difficult. I
    Couldn't really find anything to do as much
        As I had enjoined even the pursuit of
            An acting career. I tried different
    Things especially Sales, and thanks to my New York

Waitering experience, I still could get work.
It wasn't as enjoyable as it had been as
An actor in New York, knowing it
Was temporary and just a
Help along the way, while auditioning and
Having it help along the journey.
Now it was my profession and I kept trying to find
Something else to replace it.
The boys were still the joy of life
With play and now baseball and video games and
Long stretches at the Circus Arcades.
The schools in our new town of Roseville were
Great and their elementary principal
Dr. Fred Storti, had a wonderful
School at Brimhall with it's Hobbit Program and
Such great teachers like Mrs. Oswald and
Ann Hobbie.
I love all the activity with the children but financially I'm slipping.
I can't seem to get into the money making niche.
I even try multi-level marketing and it just rolls down hill
All the more into bankruptcy.

Now I am forgetting who I am.
I am forgetting my prayers, and that I chose
To come here to **remember** where I am going.
I am becoming afraid instead.
I walk out into the night alone,
I don't even see the stars,
I don't even look up. I can't even hold
My head up, I am ashamed, and
The dread begins to make
Me immobile and
I cry alone.
I forget everything and everyone.
I forget the love of my wife
And the love for my children.
I forget my Sister Mickey's love
And that she promised to
Be with me.
I forget.

CHAPTER 20: I NEED A MIRACLE

The darkness of the Night,
    The stars all cease to Shine.
The trembling of the Spirit,
    The overwhelming desire to Quit.
The panic of the Heart,
    The discovery that all is Vanity.
The laughter has ceased,
    The crime against my very own Nature.
This is the moment of my life when lack of confidence
    Overwhelms my Mind and the
        Little strength I once relied upon
            Oozes out and is poured upon an
                Insane World.
    When prayer ceased and my lips froze in Terror.
When the feeling of nothingness took over my
    Soul and I was led into the darkest of caves
        To stand alone in my darkest hour.
I rode across the country holding back the temptation
    To close my eyes and let the car plunge over
        A hill.
    I visited friends and my siblings along the way

"Where are you going everyone asked?" "To South Carolina
    And maybe a job as a singing maitre'd in a
        Beautiful restaurant," was my answer. But
            In my mind, I was saying, "I'm
                Just living out these last few days."
All along the way I remember Margaret Stephensons' words
        To me as I left on the Journey, "Expect a miracle,"
            She talked to me on the phone wishing me a good
Trip to the Ocean, but she knew I was in trouble.
        I stopped by Virginia Beach and without even
            Realizing why, I had my sister Barbara
            And her partner, Roger, take me to the
            Edgar Caycee Foundation.
I realized when I arrived and
        Went upstairs to the meditation
            Room that looked out over the
Atlantic Ocean why I had come.
    I immediately felt
My sister's presence.
        "Oh Mickey", I said,
"I have no desire to live. I need a miracle."

What happened next and continued to happen for the
   Next few days will not seem believable.
To tell you the truth, it didn't even seem believable
   To me. It was as though I was watching a
      Very good film, and was taken in hand and
         Lifted up above the Earth to
            Watch the events unfold.
I can only share with you that maybe I had already
   Lost my mind and all of this was in a temporary
      Insanity phase, or that there actually is
Divine intervention when we really need it.
   If you have had experiences that are
      In any way similar, than this
Will be a lot easier for you to believe.
   In any case I'll let you be the judge.
I felt at peace looking out over the Atlantic and after
   A while came down to the bookstore. I was
      Looking for a quote by Edgar Caycee for
         My sister Barbara, when all at once
            My hand moved to a set
Of three books all wrapped together.

They were bound in blue leather
And the gold lettering read,
"A Course in Miracles".
"That's what I need, I said, a whole course
In Miracles." I couldn't spare the $40.00
At the time, but money didn't really matter
Anymore. I just didn't think it
Really was enough to pull
Me from this pit I was slipping into.
We left the bookstore and I decided to run down
Virginia Beach along the Ocean. "I am going
To run about five miles, I told
Barb and Roger, "I'll meet you
In about 45 minutes or
So at the boardwalk."
I began my run and my thoughts went to my dear
Angel Raphael and the Book of Tobit in the
Old Testament. I felt exhilarated and
As a fine mist seem to come
Off the ocean and surround me, I used
It creatively to begin writing a screenplay about

A modern version of the ancient story.
It involved
The wonderful Angel Raphael dealing with
Tobias and Sara in Ninevah, and then
Walking through a mist on the
Sea and being in New York
With a modern couple, Toby and Sam. Sam
Being the counterpart for Sara.
I had journeyed with this wonderful angel ever since I was
A teen back at St. Raphael's parish in
Morningside, and always had a beautiful feeling of his presence when
He was near. Now the old story of how
He traveled the road with Tobias bringing
Him to finding his personal fortune, a wife called Sara,
The cure for his father, Tobit's, blindness, and
A happy life was so vivid as I ran.
Raphael always a Messenger and a Friend, was
Changing his location as he would pass
Through a mist coming off the Sea,
As I continued to create what I thought would
Make a beautiful film and maybe one
I could share with you some day.

I noticed Barbara and Roger waiting for
>Me, and they began to laugh. "Did
>>You finally take a taxi," Barbara asked?
"No, I just ran down the beach." Well it's been
>Raining like cats and dogs for over 30 minutes
>>And it just stopped. You would be
Drenched if you had run." Standing there completely
>Dry except for the perspiration of the run, I
>>Thought immediately, well if that's
>>>True then, even though I have
Decided not to live, I certainly have had one of the
>Most incredible experiences I've ever
Had while living. They walked me back to the car and
>They just smiled knowing I was trying to trick
>>Them with this tale of how I ran along the
>>>Ocean.

I am back on the road and almost to South Carolina.
>I am almost certain that I am at the end of my life.
>>I interview for the job and get it, and stay at
>>>A little beach house on the Ocean.

It was January 16th and because I had been so

Conscious of the Psalms, I began to pray
    Psalm 16, and
        I threw myself on the ground miles away from
My home and family. The Ocean that I
        Had decided to walk into to end my
    Sea of Troubles was only across a road and a sandy beach.
I lay there weeping like Aloysha in "The Brothers Karamazov."
    As I did the words of Psalm 16 now began to fill
        My head,
        Do not let me fall into the Pit,
        Let me rise and find your Path.
Now like Ishmael in Melville's wonderful novel,
    I was Lazarus. I was snatched from death.
I rose from the ground with a force of energy and a clear mind.
    I was experiencing what it was like to live after
        The Resurrection.
I heard an inner voice assure me, "You can not suffer death anymore
    You will walk away from this life,
        And Journey to a Star, to await the
            Moment of Eternity that
                Is planned for everyone."

I walked away from the beach house, the new job,
South Carolina and journeyed the next twenty-four
Hours in a car back to St. Paul
The words of Psalm 16 were still swimming in
My head, as I tried to reconstruct what happened.
Fatherly hands picked me up as I cried, I was not allowed
To fall into the Pit, and I was allowed to
Live and take the hand of my Companion
And follow His Path. I also walk with Raphael my Angel.
(See Appendix C—The Book of Tobit)
I have been on that Path for over 10 years, and no matter how desperate
Or stupid worldly situations are, I try not to fall into the
Temptation of really thinking they are anything but illusion.
I am on a Journey, without any fear of death, and I walk in Light.
It is a Light that does not fail.
It is a Light that continues to get brighter. It is a Light made from the
Specks of star dust I create as I see the insane world for what it is.
It is a Light that embraces and enfolds and allows me
To see with eyes that the Master of the New Testament promised.
It is a Light that allows me to see things that I have never seen before.

It is a Light to allow me to do even greater things than I have ever done.
It is a Light that allows me to first Heal myself, and then unites with
Others in praying for the healing, holiness and
Happiness of those around me.
It is a Light to shine upon all those who have become a part
Of my "Clusters of Friendship Groups" that have been
Assigned to us to help each other Journey to Eternity.
I stand on my Seven Story Mountain,
I hold my blue and gold volume of "A Course In Miracles"
Miraculously given to me in my moment of despair.
I walk the Path in Light discovering Happiness and
Preparing the Creation of my own Star,
By seeing the episodes of light,
And the small particles of Goodness that
Are rushing at me and allowing me to sing and laugh.
My thoughts are with my sister once again.
She is smiling and as I run along the
Ocean sides of this Journey,
She whispers for me to Remember who I am. I won't forget ever again.
I whisper back with my whole being,
"Thank you, Mickey."

CHAPTER 21: THE YEARS 1992–2001

I returned home and filled with energy like never
    Before and made the decision to move back to my
        Home town of Pittsburgh, Pennsylvania.
I walked out of the car to my sister Mary's with
    Exactly $5.00 left to my name. She advised
Me to go across the river and apply at a little restaurant
    In Aspinwall. I did and as I was asking the girl
If she would give me application to the manager or owner
    She said that the owner was standing behind me.
I turned and there was the smiling face of an old teen
    Age friend, Ray Conway. After hearing I was
Really desirous of working for him, he said "Whatever you
    Need." Ray and his wife Darlene, helped Debby and
I get back on our feet, and they are forever in my memory as
    The dearest of friends.
        The luck continued as I visited my very
Favorite gal from my childhood, Mrs. Regal and her
    Daughter Charlotte. They had a relative in human
Resources at the University of Pittsburgh, and next day
    I was hired as an Administrative Assistant there.

Now I was able to work day and night and weekends
Too and my confidence returned. I was up at
Four a.m. every morning and I was
Studying the course in miracles enthusiastically.
All of the attempts at spirituality during my life
Now seemed to make sense. I knew I was truly
On a Journey without Distance, and a
Path to my Star in the Heavens.
I sat working in the office of the Stephen Foster
Memorial and realized one day that right
Behind the wall was the stage. I had
Played on that stage in "The Tempest" with the
University of Pittsburgh Players right before
I left for New York 25 years earlier.
As I was working in the office I listened to all the
Music of Stephen Foster from many artists.
Then Dr. Root, the Curator, gave me
A recording of "Old Folks At Home" known
To most of us as "Swanee River". Only this was a very
Extraordinary piece. It was Anton Dvorak's version
A choral symphonic version that he gave as

A gift to America, just like the beautiful gift he
    Gave us of the "New World Symphony."
He had loved Pittsburgh and Erie, Pennsylvania and he
    Wrote the singing part for an Afro-American bass, Frederick T.
        Burleigh, who had guided him around the streets of
            Erie, Pennsylvania.
I was transfixed, my hands began to shake and the
    Excitement of the piece was incredible. I
        Had a vision that very first moment that
I heard it that all the people of the world were standing and
            Listening to the music of Dvorak/Foster and then
                Joined together in a Silent Prayer for Peace.
I immediately sat down and wrote a letter to President
    Clinton that I wanted this to happen for the
        Millennium at a river somewhere in the world.
I knew that someday that river could possible be the
    Tiger or Euphrates in Iraq, but I was going to
        Settle for the fact that it could begin at the
Swanee River in White Springs, Florida,
Home to another beautiful Stephen Foster Memorial.
        (See Appendix D—The Peace at Last Concert)

We had a family vote about the future and the
Debby and the guys decided they liked
Pittsburgh, but for High School they would rather return to
St. Paul and be with the friends they
Had made the years before moving to
Pittsburgh.
I was happy and spiritually very tough and said,
"Let's do it". So back to Roseville, MN, and
Roseville High School for the guys,
St. Paul's Highland High School
For Debby to interpret for Deaf students, and I
Chose to start all over once again and
Went with Northwest Airlines.
It's six years later and we have traveled to
New York to see Broadway, visited
Hawaii, Can Cun, London, Paris,
Italy, and other visits all around the country all thanks to the pass
Privilege of Northwest. Debby and I
Also worked nights and weekends at the Hilton,
Hyatt, and Holiday Inn Hotels, and even Camp Snoopy at

Our very own Mall of America.
 The boys did great in High School and moved on to the
  University of Minnesota, and both
Sean and Ryan joined Mom and Dad at the hotels working
 Evenings serving the banquets.
  I decided to become the Director of
The Peace at Last Concert at the Swanee River, and to
 Write this book. I began to see more and more
  Specks of light as I watched people respond
   To a "Hi" and a smile. I began to
    See miracles in my life and
In the lives of those that I promised to join with in
 Prayer.
When I finish this book I am going to put together a book of
 Daily readings from some of the most inspiring
  Spiritual literature of all times.
   I am a happy man.
  I love that I have raised two sons that are
Absolutely incredible. They make me laugh, they scare
 Me with their acts of courage, they inspire me with
Their youth and their search for the right vocation.

I love traveling to New York and seeing Broadway. Generally,
My dear niece Michelle DiBucci and her partner Ed Bilous
Get us house seats for the best shows. They have a
Music company in New York and make music for commercials.
They also teach at Julliard, and Michelle never stops
Working creatively on magnificent pieces of
Music in that she is an avant garde
Classical composer.
The very first trip back to New York and to begin this
This new tradition of flying in from St. Paul to
See the shows, was to see Carol Burnett
Return to Broadway after 30 years in a comedy called
"Moon over Buffalo". We had house seats thanks
To Carol and permission to stop back stage
Following the play.
My sons and Debby always admired the
Photograph the living room of
Me standing with Carol and Dick Van Dyke,
When they did "Same Time, Next Year." However,
It was now about twenty years since that
Moment, and there I was standing in the green room waiting

With others to see Carol. Eunice Shriver and her daughter,
    Marisa Shriver, wife of Arnold Schwartneggar were
        There and the boys could hardly believe they
            Were standing beside the wife of the
                Their wonderful cinema star,
                    Arnold Schwatsneggar.
Carol arrived and immediately began to shake the hands
    Of the celebrities and friends who had also seen
        The show and were showering her with
            Praise and fond kudos.
All of a sudden I realized her back was to us and
    Seemingly we had been ignored from the
        Activities. Just for a moment I felt
The pain of what it would be like if she left, and never
    Even said hello to the family. It was at that moment
        However, that the room became very quiet
            As Carol turned around and faced
The four of us and just looked at us. She then opened
    Her arms wide and as she approached me,
        She said in her most wonderful
            Burnett-resonant tones,

"and Don."
She came up to me and hugged me warmly and talked
About how long it had been since our
Work together. She talked with my
Family and they were all excited to meet this
Wonderful woman who brought such laughter to the world.
We left the theatre and the boys ran ahead,
Smiling. Dad had received a
Big hug from this big star.
It was a big hug, Carol; it was worth being in
Show business for a few moments of my
Life with one of the Stars of our
Times. I glanced up at the
Winter sky and the
Stars as we walked to Sardi's for
Dinner. I couldn't even hold
Back my exclamation as I held Debby's hand
And glad to be walking the streets of Broadway
After so many years.
In my happiness, all I could say was
"Thank you, Carol."

CHAPTER 22: THE PEACE AT LAST CONCERT

I had a vision of the World at Peace in 1992. In 1996
I watched the Olympics Opening Ceremonies and
Wrote what I thought was an introduction to
This book but made it part of the Appendix.
In 1999 I decided to at least begin with two people,
Myself and my wife Debby, and go to the
Swanee River in Florida and hold the
First Peace at Last Concert.
I was working at the Hilton at my moonlighting job of
Banquet waitering telling a co-worker, Amy Haen that
I was going to bring in the 20th
Century with the banquet and I wanted as many people
Like she to join with me in Spirit. She immediately
Responded to the idea and said she would be
With me in spirit. "I wish I didn't
Have to work on New Year's Eve, but at a hotel
There's no getting out of the 'ol New Year's Eve
Celebrations especially this one with
The year 2000 coming." I understood
What Amy was going through for as a waiter in New York, I had

Done my share of the New Years parties. Sometimes
I was in the midst of doing a play and that was nice, but the
Best memories had been when I just treated it as
A very spiritual and quiet beginning to a new
Year.
About 200 people friends, family and co-workers
Joined Debby and I when we did the Peace at Last Program.
The following year 2001 and the official
Millenium we held it again and this time we had 500
And in 2002 a 1000 joined us in spirit from all over the
U.S. and Italy and Germany.
The program was the Foster Dvorak Symphonic
Choral arrangement of "Old Folks at Home" (Swanee River), and the poetry of
Maya Angelou and Walt Whitman.
(See Appendix D—Peace at Last)
It was interesting that this time I invited
Hillary Clinton and she sent along best wishes, as did
Mayou Angelou who gave permission for the
Reading of her beautiful poem.
A nice discovery at this time was a quote from a professor at
Stanford University. (See Preface) He said when people

Have the same thought at the same time. The number is not 200
But 200 squared or 40,000. And then when
It was 500 people it was like having
The force of 250,000.
So I will continue to go to the shores of the Swanee
Each year with the hope that the entire
World will some day join in for
Five minutes of silence for
Peace.
If only for a brief moment that we all embrace
Our world in silence and in love. The
Planets will shift and a path will be unfolded
Leading to heaven. When all voices of the
World give thanks for peace at the
Same time it will truly be
Peace at Last.

CHAPTER 23: A NEW VISION

A New heaven and a New earth
    A Place where children are free to Play
        A Land that shares its wealth with other lands
An End to bigotry, injustice, hatred and war and
    The final days of conduct unbecoming the
        Sons of God.
An Acceptance of other people, their cultures
    And most of all their religions.
A New beginning, a song of joy played
    Throughout the world
A Dance of celebration as the trumpets
    Blast out for the stars to hear.
A World of Happiness for every child of God
    A Song of praise to the Stars that
        Shine out as we walk our Path to Eternity.

CHAPTER 24: WHEN I WALK AWAY

I want you to be there when
  I walk away from this earth.
I want you to have proof that I
  Shared with you this powerful moment.
  I want you to be with me on
March 2, 2033 as I walk to the stars on my path made
  Of the star dust of my life.
    I am not quite sure yet if I will
      Go the mountains and run away
    As a deer.
Or if I'll go to Brazil and stand like the statue
  With my arms extended out to the sky.
I may walk along the Ocean and this time the mist
  Will envelop me and take me away, rather than
  Extend to me the resurrection of life it
    Gave me that day I became
    Lazarus re-born.
I can feel the warmth of the sun already, and
  The sand particles are shining like Star
  Dust.

If it's night I know I will not only see, but
I will hear the Stars.
It will be that final standing
Ovation for a wonderful performance and
I'll take my final curtain call.
I have not figured out all of this yet,
So until the future becomes the
Now I Journey with, know that we Journey together
On these starry nights.
When you feel your "powerful self"
Remember me.
I was just a deer and a
Gump in the Forest who
Pierced the Mystery of Life.
I extend my hands and I wave to you and
As I do particles of light continue to remind
Me of you and that you are my Brother, and
That we are
One.
As for me—I discovered that—
It takes star dust to create a star.

APPENDIX A—A LETTER FROM A MONTGOMERY JAIL

The Duquesne University Commentator, March, 1965

Dear Fellow Students,

Unaccustomed as I am to writing from jail, I still feel the need to communicate some of my recent experiences to you. I am very proud and happy about all the news I have received from Duquesne University. I feel that the money contributed and the concern extended is much more than I deserve, but I appreciate it. It comes as a real uplifter of spirit, since I have found times here when discouragement and despair have tried to tempt me. I realize my body is weak since I have been on a hunger strike with the forty-five other college students in this cell since Thursday. It is now six days later.

I would like to tell you what had happened since I came, why I did come, and why I'm glad I'm here.

I left Sunday night, March 14th, from Pittsburgh with the Pittsburgh Friends of SNCC (Student Non-Violent Coordinating Committee). Forty students from Pitt, Chatham, Carnegie Tech, Mt. Mercy and Duquesne University filled the first of 3 buses. Chick Strain, Jim Peay and myself represented Duquesne.

The trip was one of great spirit for the 850 mile, 23 hour ride through the South. The singing of freedom songs filled the air, as sandwiches were prepared and passed around.

In Birmingham, where we had a rest stop, we felt that the Southern white citizen was not happy with our presence. Having stayed in the South these past two week, I realize how much we must come to understand the position of this person. His way of life has been entirely upset by the Negroes' move for equality, and he cannot fully understand what is going on. The presence of students from all over the country has perplexed as well as embittered him. Personally, I can see the real need for establishing meaningful ways of dialogue and communication between the responsible while community and the responsible Negro community. This appeal has not really been made, and I see it as one of the necessary and crucial efforts that must be made. But many Southern whites have agreed that there has been injustice, and that inflicting death and injury is their crime. They acknowledge their guilt, especially, by failing to speak forthrightly in defense of human rights and justice for all.

For many of the students, one could see that a big reason for their involvement was the fact that they did not want to stand silent on an issue that had cried for the response of all mankind, let alone American citizens. Wolfgang Mathissen, a student from the University of Pittsburgh and a citizen of West Germany, said in a workshop in the Negro community of Montgomery our first day here, "People from Germany were silent while the Jewish people were slain. We must never allow this to ever occur again."

We arrived in Montgomery on Monday, March 15th about 9:00 PM, and immediately went on a picket to the State Capitol. We were stopped a few blocks short of the Capitol by the police, and so we sat in protest for about two hours. We returned with hundreds of other students from all over the country to the South Jackson Street Baptist Church. This was SNCC headquarters for the Montgomery project, and was part of the Negro community. We knew it was a poorer part of town because the sidewalks turned from cement to dirt. This was as strange as the water fountains in City Hall labeled "colored" and "white". We have segregated areas in

Pittsburgh, but the distinction is not so vividly drawn. The Negro community of South Jackson Street prepared food for us that evening. We from Pittsburgh joined many fellow students and slept on the floor of the overcrowded Baptist Church.

Tuesday, March 16, proved to be the most eventful and tragic day of the trip. That morning we marched to schools of the nearby neighborhood to recruit High School students and students from Alabama State College to join the march and picket at the Capitol. With these Negro students and men and women from northern universities, we began a four to five hundred strong march. Again, we were stopped a few blocks from the Capitol by the city police. We sat down and in about an hour more students arrived, but were not allowed to join our group, which was surrounded by police on the sidewalk opposite us.

Not long after this, a posse on horseback from the Sheriff's Office, led by state trooper, rode into the students standing across the street. They routed them by beating them with clubs. One girl, Pam Clemson, from Juniata College, was surrounded by three horsemen and she refused to move. They poked her in the ribs trying to get her away from the tree she had braced herself against. The cowboys weren't so gentle with the male students. A Japanese student from the University of Pennsylvania went down and wouldn't move. He was clubbed a few more time and finally sprawled out unconscious. The horsemen now turned their attention to the huge group across the street. They rode directly into the crowd swinging their clubs. The line fell back and began to walk away, but the horsemen kept on the heels of those in the rear swinging their clubs till there was a panic-stricken crowd now hurrying back toward the Negro community

Fritz Kraal, from Amherst, staying in the rear of the line and received two blows which started blood rolling down his head over his face. He never went into a panic and kept his protective position. Chuck Strain, a Duquesne Graduate Student, and my friend in this cell, stopped to help a student who had fallen. He felt the shoe of a horse against his own and retreated with the student to safety. Other male students sheltered female students and hurried them out of the way of the oncoming cattle horses rode by a callused and frightening crew. They turned and let us go on once we arrived in the vicinity of the Negro community.

To say that people were in a state of shock and puzzlement is to minimize the state that existed. Speeches were immediately given by the SNCC leaders and to many the atmosphere of violence and a possible race riot seemed to be in the air. Neither of these occurred, and to one understanding the civil rights non-violent movement, the speeches did not incite to fear. Despite remarks made by Rabbi Rubenstein of Pitt, many realized this and were ready to hold ground with the Montgomery community. Rabbi Rubbenstien is not able to really comment on the Alabama situation. He went home too frightened.

Jim Foreman, a great and able leader of SNCC, spoke to the Pittsburgh groups attempting to dispel the fears of violence. He asked for their regaining strength and remaining with the Negro community that had been awakened to a call of action from the presence of so many students from the North. That night, one hundred of the one hundred thirty Pittsburgh students returned home. By Saturday, there were only seven students remaining.

Martin Luther King arrived that evening and spoke to the community at the Buelah Baptist Church. He said that many people were wondering when he and all these students would be satisfied. He answered, "Not until all men can wear the shoes of dignity and equality." He announced he would lead a march the following day to the Courthouse to protest the use of such violence by the posse. The following morning, the march led by Reverend King went to the Montgomery Courthouse. The crowd numbered about four thousand and waited three hours in a drenching storm. Everyone was soaked through to the skin, yet they awaited the return of Reverend King. He returned with the news that the Selma to Montgomery March had just been approved, and that he had to return to the sheriff's office for further negotiations. Later that night, he returned with Jim Foreman and a few students and after a five-hour meeting, received a guarantee by the Sheriff that unnecessary violence would not be resorted to again. They also agreed that for further demonstrations, the marchers would secure a parade permit.

Thursday morning, Jim Foreman of SNCC announced that peaceful pickets were not considered demonstrations. He said that the right for peaceful assembly was guaranteed by the first amendment to the Constitution and did not need to have people engaged in this activity secure a parade permit.

Pickets left the church for the Capitol all day, and they were arrested. Friday, more pickets were planned and Wolfgang Mathiesen and I joined one planned for 4:00 PM.

Some forty students, including Chick Strain from Duquesne University, were already in city jail, and the sent word from jail that they had begun a hunger strike: 1.) to protest the arrest, and 2.) to protest that they were put in segregated cells separated from the Negro students that were arrested with them.

At 4:00 PM, Wolfgang led the pickets to the Capitol. We carried signs saying "One Man—One Vote—Register to Vote". State troopers stood on the edge of the sidewalk surrounding the Capitol. Wolfgang continued to ask them to let him by so as to get on the sidewalk. The captain in charge refused. When asked why, he said, "because I say so." The city police arrived and surrounded us on the outside giving the order for us to get off the street and on to the sidewalk. Wolf delivered continuous pleas to the state troopers who would not let us off the street. The chief of police announced that we were under arrest for disobeying a lawful order, and we were thrown in vans and taken to jail.

Montgomery City Jail was overcrowded when we arrived, and so we were sent to an extension of Kilby Prison, used by the Montgomery Police in emergencies. We were fifty strong in a huge cell. The Negroes, directly across the way numbered sixty. We supported the idea of the hunger strike, and we set about pooling cigarettes, cough drops and vitamin pills that could be used for those who grew weak. Into the fifth day of the hunger strike we lost four students who were directed to eat by a doctor since they had previous medical records and that this might be too injurious to them. The morale of the men remained high during all of this.

Sunday morning, A Reverend John Hallsten, Lutheran Chaplain at Colorado State, held devotional service. All of the Negroes joined in, but only fifteen of the white students. According to a survey made by a graduate student in Sociology at John Hopkins, Lou Goldberg, of the men in jail about two-thirds professed to be agnostic or atheistic. Yet, these men displayed a love for mankind and dedication to justice and freedom that would certainly impress anyone of a Christian background. I will never be able to forget the light illuminated and the love exhibited by these students who professed agnosticism and atheism.

Having covered what has happened since I've been here, I would like to relate why I did decide to come, and why I am glad I did come. Since the March on Washington in 1963, I have become more and more aware of the racial issue in Pittsburgh as well as in the South. During these last couple of years, I have worked in racial affairs and have discussed the problems on a national as well as a community scale. I also presided over Duquesne University's Council of Interracial Friendship. It has been during this time that I have become more convinced that racial equality, freedom for all men, and the extinction of racial prejudice, are issues I cannot remain silent on. I feel deep inside that I must make my stand and my witness for something I believe to be truth.

When I head about the Selma tragedy, I was sick. On the Saturday after the Reverend Reeb's death, I attend a memorial service held at the University of Pittsburgh in the Heinz Chapel. While in meditation, I felt that I must answer a call within me to express my concern for our people in Alabama. I didn't know how exactly, but when I heard about the SNCC call for students and the bus leaving from Pittsburgh, I immediately accepted. I was well aware this was not a vacation to the South. I was a little frightened that possibly my own life would be in danger, yet I knew I had to be part of the front line. I had to back up a couple of years of dialogue with the giving of myself to the Civil Rights battle.

I am glad I came. Over and over I heard from Negroes of Montgomery that they were glad I had come. The phrase, "I'm sure glad you al are here," range in my ears and became inscribe on my heart. I couldn't return to Pittsburgh immediately after the first crisis because I had fallen in love with the people. I knew that my presence even for a few days more was worth gold to them.

These people treated me with great respect and admiration. I talked with them into the early ours of the morning on the whole subject of freedom and equality. Despite what others may say—the Negro of the South does want his freedom, and does not want a second-class citizenship. He had begun to be awakened to the fact that the time has come for his involvement and that he can no longer be silent while prejudice, injustice and hate reign. One of the most impressive statements that I heard over and over was: "If you people from the North care enough for us and our cause to come down here and place yourselves in dangerous positions, then it is time we began to really get behind our leaders and fight (non-violently) for freedom." We all agreed that someday—We Shall Overcome.

I hope each of you reflects on what your position has been in this struggle whether at home, on campus, or in Alabama. I pray that you come to an awareness of the problem and form a conscience as well as a stand of conviction for all our brothers—Black and White.

In Friendship,
Don R. McGrath, A'65

Editor's Note: Mr. McGrath wrote this letter while on a hunger strike in jail.

APPENDIX B—POETRY 1974–2000

Knight of Existence (Part I—Night of Knights)

Obviously not interested…

No electricity…and

I find myself yawning and

Stretching and saying "Have a good-nite"…while

Underneath I question this lack of energy—this

Non-spark—when seemingly one would think it would be

There—that one being me.

Who is to challenge the inability?

To rush

To rape

To ravage

The beauty that might exist and yet so easily be

Destroyed the Don Juanismic leap into the life of

Another.

So with acceptance with nonchalance thee is

Only a greeting

Only a sigh

Only a cliché and then a

Good night and the days

Pass that are really years—the

Struggle for finding

The love

The other

In all the existences of those I know continues.

Then with a warning like a sob that comes in a

Cinema verite'

The Truth emerges during the laugh,

During the hysterical melting of souls

That can not be explained

And who is to explain

The mystery of the laugh

Of the joy

Of the sharing

Of the coughing, the choking

The heavy breathing

The convulsions of comedy

That comes from the Camarada of a Saturday afternoon

Then nothing?

Are you serious?

Hearts begin to take that long celestial

Journey toward one another

Both different

Both apart

Different lives that again seemingly have no

Relationship at all in this Universe of chance

But because of the beauty of the unknown

And because of the divinity of the mysterious

There is an avalanche of happenings that are like the

Snows of an uncontrolled mountain of emotion.

It begins with simple reason

A smile, a friend, a caring, a sharing and then a

Night of existence while

Aeons of moments race by

We race to climb the Mountain of Ourselves.

Reflections on the window and

Fingers entwined

We are transported to a land of trees and

While walking discover the twilight of

Autumn.

There is no escape from falling leaves so there is also

No escape from that which was meant to be.
So good friends toast and seem to affirm
The existence of something very special
That appears so rarely during the course of life.
So thoughts continue like year-like days and the
Charge is felt in the electricity that had been
Hiding in streams since the beginning, and the
Vibrant light—the affirmation of beings has its birth.
How will it continue?
How will it keep its intensity?
Plugged into only the Loveliness of the Now?
The answer is in the need, the necessity, the
Beauty of the collage of suffering, pain, joy and laughter
That led to the evolution of this
Eden.
And as the group sways and the
Party swings the
Society of Life demand the ordinary
But
You're own inability to conform
Allows you to
"Clap with your feet" and

Dance the only Dance there is—the song of laughter

Dying only with a smile caught in your throat—and the

Electric nights of existence begin.

Music plays; couples undulate and in the sweat are

Vows that life is all noise drowning out the

Sweet melodies of feeling your own pain…

You choose the

Upper Room, the quiet room, the inner room

Where bread was broken and wine was shared by the

Disciples of dialogues and stories and

Failing to achieve the winning approval of the

Noisy din of dens outside that tiny cosmos they kneel together.

As others seek the night of Knights you have found the

Holy Grail and you are crowned

King and Queen and run to your castle of dreams.

Part II—Castle of Dreams

Across the moat they rode and

Closed the castle doors

This fair Guinevere and her Lancelot,

In Camelot the Round Table cheered and

Hailed their Damsel and their Dane.

Life continued....

The Journey toward each other

The giving of the Road

The clearing of the Way

What poured from their hearts?

Sparkled in their eyes with a

Glow that would light the Path

They celebrated everything...

Feasts, holidays, holy days and the

Anniversary of their births.

They began to discover they hid things

They deeply felt...

But ready for Virtue the lovers under

A darkened sky drew apart and

It rained reality.

Coming together again they made a vow

Not to Let the Sun go down.

Snows of holidays

Divided kingdoms

The bitter sweet revelation of separation

A challenge of Truth and Time.

Back again to the castle

To dream together while

Cupid repaired their vine with new beginnings…

Golden pencils

Rabbits

Flags and the

Lute…gifts of reason and of rhyme.

Suddenly, a

Grey cloud, a black sky

There was no robin singing outside the

Castle walls.

Into the night of Existence our Knight rode out

Alone…

Alone into days of lonely nights

Into the adjoining kingdoms of Doubt

Searching an unsure universe for the

Holy Grail—the Lost Self.

Like a prodigal Son that from

A father free

He ran into harlots of torment

Drinking the bitter wine that poured from his eyes.

Camelot was silent

Sadness hung like empty goblets

Round a Table that had no Chairs.
Now our Knight a little older
Crossed the Bridge of Success
While reality rained for Seven Days and
Seven Nights and while sitting in their loneliness
Two Lovers now strangers meet again to
Discover they both were
There…
Ready to ride slowly back to their Kingdom but
Riding Oh so softly over the
Steps of each other's minds.
They stop in the
Garden outside those dream doors
To patch the wounds of heartfelt scars
In their war for Peace
Where battles are never ended
In the life long struggle of
A Man and a Woman
A Knight and a Lady
A King and a Queen
They go to the Chapel of the Resurrection for the
Communion of their souls—and climbing the

Mountains of themselves they come to the Castle of Dreams,

And love comes once again.

Part III—Climbing the Mountains of Ourselves

With Love there is discovery

With Love there is Joy
                Pain
                    Doubt
                        Awareness

With Love there is an Ascent.

And so Upwards our Lovers strove

As daily they reached for each other

Living together they reached for themselves.

A Castle they were given, a Camelot was theirs

Together they ruled their private Kingdom.

As nights continued this Knight and his Lady

Reigned over their Castle of Dreams.

Fantasy and reality a mixture of

Heaven and Hell is living

Together and Caring
                Laughing
                      Acting
                          Singing
                              Fighting
                                  Sharing

In a single word
              Loving.
Outside the castle walls in the bushes of
Everyday life the enemies of Togetherness
Sleep always with one eye open listening
Without despair for the crevices in this pair.
Undaunted our courtly couple found that
They must always be Vigilant
They must keep the Candles of Memories lit
Never forgetting their early years when they
Clapped with their feet.
They slipped by the foes of
Sickness and exhaustion who constantly
Wait and repaired themselves by visits to
Oceans of rest.
That confidence fantastic and freshly
Restored this beauty and mate and they
Returned to the reality of everyday living
Ready to meet the foes at the Gate.
These devils just praying for Fate to lose
Her sense of Humor and let our lovers
Lose ground to those beings of Evil.

Laughter and Smiles were like arrows

Into the deepest sinew of depression and

These enemies were slain by maturity and

Grace when what they had planned was

Mere regression.

Side by Side in the day and in the

Night armored with the strength of Self and Other

Came to defeat their bitter foes.

The found direction in dialogue and

Courage in sharing their thoughts and

They put away the Temptation to travel alone and so

Together they kept the watch till Dawn.

Leaning on each other both with

Inner strength independent in thought and action

Yet dependent on each other's kindness and gentleness and

Love they whisper final words before the Breath of Sleep and

The Mirrors of their Minds reflect their

Morning Psalm
        Climb Me!
            Climb up My Love!
                      Climb the Mountain of Yourself!

Running for America

I am running along the Ocean
People fill the beach—Black and White and Tan, Young and Old
It is a Happy Day—a big Birthday Party—and it's for America!
I am running by the hotel, the motel, and the
Houses and apartments that line the ocean streets.
TV sets are tuned in to the President talking about what
We still as a Nation must do, and while we begin our
Third Century, a child called Elizabeth is born and
Crying out on NBC making her television debut.
People on porches watch the Hudson vibrate with the sailing ships, a
Birthday gift from England, Denmark, Argentina,
Rumania, Russia, Germany, Chile, Italy and Japan all
Smiling at the Eagle, the ship, the bird and the land.
I am running with ecstasy today, a Marathon of Joy and
Kinship with that first marathon runner of Athens and
All who have ever run to cry out Victory! Freedom! Liberte'!
The grandest birthday party in the peaceful history of Mankind
Continues as I move on thrilled but with nothing more to say
I am applauding, smiling, laughing, and I am breathless that
I am running for America today.   (July 4, 1976, the Bicentennial Year)

Peacocks on the Snow

As white cold flurries fly fitfully

In the ice cold deep of the city and

Chills unfelt by both my

Body and spirit until now possess me

I walk slowly out of the great stone

Edifice built for that one hour of

Worship where I hid from my

Neighbor in my effort to commune with my God.

The poor outside chant "no" to the

Peaceful service and to the

Eviction notice written on the

Doors of their futures

"Don't disrupt our Service" cries the

High Priest, "this is our one hour with

God" cries a lay official,

"How dare you disturb our tranquillity"?

My shame is a cancer within me

Gnawing at the comfortable lining of

My being as intellectual participant

"Get out of our Church"

"Get off our sidewalks"
"Don't remind us that our problems
Are as near at the front gate"
"We have Jazz Concerts to
Schedule and
We've helped you once"
"Forgive us our trespasses" we all in
Unison voice as the chant of poverty and
Homelessness will not go away.
"If Christ came down he would smash this
Temple" says a poor representative of the
People of the Eviction.
"We know the Gospel" scream the holy men of
God, "don't preach during our coffee hour."
The banquet is over and I leave
My lips purple with the stains of
Him who taught me to take the poor
Unto my heart while the cold is as
Still as a frame of film that moves
Speedily on like time.
I look for Beauty and as in a Fairy Tale
Three Peacocks walk by me on the snow.

The Prince of the Long Journey

If you listen closely you can still hear
Footsteps continuing to ring down the
Halls where he walked his last miles

A long life, a good life, a life filled
With many memories as a gentle nurse
Protects him on his daily promenade

Echo upon echo of footsteps back through
History and years of believing, fighting
Hoping that revolution would bring peace.

It is a long way back through the paths of
Time to see and hear the injustice when
Man turns against man brother against brother.

Back to when with light of candle he
Searched for the good and the beautiful
A searcher of truth with words and thoughts

No man of quiet desperation no life wasted
While long years of dedicated hours to the
Family of man our dear brother toiled in love

And we the family benefit by this genius

This elevation of cosmic consciousness

This phenomenon of man this continual ascent

Spiraling upward and always evolving to that

Divinity to which we all aspire that birthright

Seen by those with special vision and blessed eyes

This brother philosopher lived for with his

Gifts of mind and spirit which were like the

Mortar of the foundation of the house of man

And in his home within that circle of love

His brother of mercy and sister of charity

With all his family and dedicated friends

Listen closely now as the footsteps down the hall

Remind then that the prince of the long journey

Keeps walking always in the memories of our hearts

The Prince of the Long Journey was written in memory of Aaron Kravitz on July 22,

1977, for my voice teacher and friend Harold Kravitz, who sang as Harold Kravitt, and

Was generous beyond belief to his students who loved him as he taught them up to his

Own 90th birthday, and who only paused during the day or interrupted a voice lesson to

Walk Aaron down the halls of their New York apartment on West 79th street.

Our Boy, my Love!

He is pure, Precious, an Angel
    He is Laughter from its source
        He is Joy incarnate

He is a bubble of joy, a Sea of happiness
    A Prayer—transcendental and euphoric

He sails over our consciousness
    He dives into our beings
        He leaves our lives breathless

He is Humanity
    A host of valuable whales and tender baby seals

He is a circus of continuity
    He is so clown like in his expansiveness
        He is a ringleader of total captivity

He cries only refreshing rain
    He smiles sunny waves of nights and days
        He sleeps—a sculpture of contented dreams

He is a tiny prince of poetic garbling
    A Creator of a Garden and the Tree of Caress
        Filled with babbling pink and yellow bluebirds.

                —For Debby, January 15, 1981

On The Road Of Life

I was walking down a Road by myself

The Road happened to meander through the streets of New York

It continued through a Beautiful Park

Central to the City

And for me it was the Center of the Universe.

I was okay

But I was alone…

I continued my walk to the Hudson

Where I looked up and out over the River.

On the side of the Hill

There was a Tree

Midst stones planted to memories of transitions.

Under the Tree

Covered with Silver Apples of the Moon and

Golden Apples of the Sun

There sat a Queen of the Night.

Her names was Debbie…

She spoke to me of Love and of

Finding a friend

On the Road of Life.

She said is was time…

Time to Take the Hand of a

Traveler who would smell of Hazelnuts then she

Smiled as the Sun went down and the

Moon came up over the park

Central to the City…

I walked home.

It was turning towards a New Day and the

Epiphany Feast had begun—a

Manifestation of the mixture of

Broadway lights and star Light that

Lit my Way.

It was the last era that

I was to spend Alone for the next

Morning I Ran into the Dawn of Discovery and a

Friend—her name was Debby…

She smiled

She twinkled like the stars

She was diamonds in jeans and I crowned her

Queen of a New Day.

The Journey down the

Tracks of Discovery had begun

We were ready to run the Race.

We would be friends forever

On The Road Of Life.

—The Feast of Epiphany (21 years later), January 6, 2000

APPENDIX C—THE BOOK OF TOBIT

The Book of Tobit—the story of Tobias & Sara brought together by the Angel Raphael.

This book follows the book of Nehemiah, and is the Jerusalem Bible (translation of 1966) with permission of double day.

The Book of Tobit. (excerpts)

Chapter 1

I, Tobit, have walked in paths of truth and in good works all the days of my life. I have given much in alms to my brothers and fellow countrymen, exiled like me in Nineveh in the country of Assyria. (Chapter 1)

Chapter 2

And I wept. When the sun was down, I went and dug a grave and buried him. My neighbors laughed and said, "See, he is not afraid any more. (You must remember that a price had been set on my head earlier for this very thing.) "The time before he had to flee, yet here he is, beginning to bury the dead again."

That night I took a bath; then I went into the courtyard and lay down by the courtyard wall. Since it was hot I left my face uncovered. I did not know that there were sparrows in the wall above my head; their hot droppings fell into my eyes. White spots then formed, which I was obliged to have treated by the doctors. But the more ointments they tried me with, the more the spots blinded me, and in the end I became blind altogether. I sighed and wept, and prayed:

> Lord, I wait for the sentence you will give to deliver me from this affliction. Let me go away to my everlasting home; do not turn your face from me. For it is better to die than still to live in the face of of trouble that knows no pity; I am weary of hearing myself traduced.

Chapter 3

It chanced on the same day that Sarah who lived in Media, also heard insults from one of her father's maids. You must know that she had been given in marriage seven times, and that Asmodeus, the worst of demons, had killed her bridegrooms one after another before ever they slept with her as man and wife. The servant girl said, "Just because your bridegrooms have died, that is no reason for punishing us. Go and join them, and may we be spared the sight of any child of yours." That day she grieved and with outstretched arms she prayed:

> You are blessed, O God of Mercy! Already I have lost seven husbands; why should I live any longer? If it does not please you to take my life, Then look on me with pity; I can myself traduced no longer.

Chapter 4

The same day, Tobit remembered the silver that he had left with Gabael at Rhages in Media and summoned Tobias his son and told him.

Chapter 5

Tobias went out to look for a man who knew the way to go with him to Media. Outside he found Raphael the angel standing facing him (though he did not guess it was an angel of God). Tobias asked: "Do you know the road to Media? The other replied: "Certainly I do".

Chapter 6

Tobias left with the angel, and the dog followed behind. The two walked on, and when the evening came they camped beside the Tigris. They caught a fish and the angel said, "cut it open, and take out the gall, heart and liver for they have curative properties. You burn the heart and the liver in case a person is plagued by a demon. As regards the gall, this is used as an eye ointment for anyone having white spots on the eyes; after using it, you only have to blow on the spots to cure them.

Chapter 7

At Raguel's house they washed and bathed and sat down to table. Tobias immediately fell in love with Sarah and asked for her hand in marriage. Raguel, said, "I must be frank with you. I have tried to find a husband for her seven times among our kinsmen, and all of them have died the first evening, on going to her room. But for the present, my boy, eat and drink; and the Lord will grant you his grace and peace." Tobias, spoke out, "I will not hear of eating and drinking till you have come to a decision about me." Raguel answered, "Very well. Since, as prescribed by the Book of Moses, she is given to you, heaven itself decrees she shall be yours. I therefore entrust your sister to you. From now you are her brother and she is your sister. She is given to you from today forever. The Lord of heaven favor you tonight, my child, and grant you his grace and peace. Raguel called for his daughter Sarah, took her by the hand and gave her to Tobias with these words, "I entrust her to you, the law and the ruling recorded in the Book of Moses assign her to you as your wife. Take her; take her home to your father's house with a good conscience. The God of heaven grant you a good journey in peace." Then he turned to her mother, Edna, for the writing paper. He drew up the marriage contract , how he gave his daughter as bride to Tobias according to the ordinance in the Law of Moses.

After this they began to eat and drink Raguel called his wife Edna and said, "My sister, prepare the second room and take here there." She went and made the bed in this room as he had ordered, and took her daughter to it. She wept over her, then wiped away her tears and said, Courage, daughter!" and she went out.

Chapter 8

When they had finished eating and drinking and it seemed time to go to bed, the young man was taken from the dining room to the bedroom. Tobias remembered Raphael's advice; he went to his bag, took the fish's heart and liver out of it and put some on the burning incense. The reek of the fish distressed the demon, who fled through the air to Egypt. Raphael pursued him there, and bound and shackled him at once.

The parents meanwhile had gone out and shut the door behind them. Tobias rose from the bed, and said to Sarah, "Get up, my sister! You and I must pray and petition our Lord to win his grace and his protection. She stood up, and they began praying for protection, and this was how they began:

> You are blessed, O god of our fathers;
> Blessed, too, is your name
> For ever and ever.
> Let the heavens bless you and
> All things you made for evermore.

> It was you who created Adam,
> You who created Eve his wife
> To be his help and support; and from these
> Two the human race was born.
> It was you who said,
> *"It is not good that the man should be alone;*
> *Let us make him a helpmate like himself."*
> And so I do not take my sister
> For any lustful motive;
> I do it in singleness of heart.
> Be kind enough to have pit on her and on me and
> Bring us to old age together.

And together they said, "Amen, Amen", and lay down for the night.

But Raguel rose and called his servants, who came and helped him to dig a grave. He had thought, "Heaven grant he does not die! We should be overwhelmed with ridicule and shame." When the grave was finished, Raguel went back to the house, called his wife, and said, "Will you send a maid to the room to see if Tobias is still alive" For if He is dead, we may be able to bury him without anyone else knowing."

The maid was called the lamp lit and the door opened; the maid went it. She found the two fast asleep; she came out again and whispered. "He is not dead, all is well." Then Raguel blessed the God of heaven with these words:

> You are blessed, my God,
> With every blessing that is pure;
> May you be blessed for evermore!

> You are blessed for having made me glad.
> What I feared has not happened;
> Instead you have treated us with
> Mercy beyond all measure.

> You are blessed for taking pity
> On this only son, this only daughter.
> Grant them, Master, your grace and protection;
> Let them live out their lives
> In happiness and in grace.

And he made his servants fill the grave in before dawn broke.

He told his wife to make plenty of bread, he went to his flock, brought back two oxen and four sheep and gave orders for them to be cooked; and preparations began. He called Tobias and said, "I will not hear of you leaving here for a fortnight. You are to stay where you are, eating and drinking, with me. You will make my daughter happy again after all her troubles. After that, take away a half of all I have and go without hindrance back to your father. When my wife and I are dead you will have the other half. Courage, my boy! I am your father, and Edna is your mother. We are your parents in future, as we are your sister's. Courage, my Son!

Chapter 9

Then Tobias turned to Raphael, and said, "Brother Azarias, take four servants and two camels and leave for Rhages. Go to Gabael" house, give him the receipt and see about the money; then invite him to come with you to my wedding feast. You know that my father must be counting the days and that I cannot lost a single one without worrying him.

Chapter 10

After 14 days of feasting. Raguel said to Tobias these parting words, "Good health my son, and a happy journey! May the lord of heaven be gracious to you and to your wife, Sarah! I hope to see your children before I die. To his daughter, Sarah he said, "Go now to your father-in-law's house, since henceforward they are as much your parents as those who gave you life. Go in peace, my daughter, I hope to hear nothing but good of you, as long as I live"

Edna in her turn said to Tobias, "Dear son and brother, may it please the Lord to bring you back again! I hope to live long enough to see the children of you and Sara before I die. In the sight of the Lord I give my daughter into your keeping. Never make her unhappy as long as you live. Go in peace, my son. Henceforward I am your mother and Sarah is your sister. May we all live happily all the days of our lives!" And she kissed them both and saw them set our happily. Tobias waved goodbye and gave his blessing to Raguel and his wife Edna, "May it be my happiness to honor you all the days of my life."

Chapter 11

Raphael said to Tobias before he reached his father, "I give you my word that your father's eyes will open. You must put the fish's gall to his eyes, the medicine will smart and will draw a filmy white skin off his eyes. And your father will be able to see and look on the light.

Anna was sitting, watching the road, and said to Tobit, "here comes your son, with his companion. She ran forward and threw her arms round her son's neck. "Now I can die", she said, "I have seen you again". And she wept. Tobit rose to his feet and stumbled across the courtyard through the door. Tobias came on towards him (he had the fish's gall in his hand). He blew into his eyes and said, steadying him, "Take courage, father!" With this he applied the medicine, left it there awhile, then with both hands peeled away a filmy skin from the corner of his eyes. Then his father fell on his neck and wept. He exclaimed, "I can see, my son, the light of my eyes! And he said:

> Blessed be God!
> Blessed be his great name!
> Blessed be all his holy angels!

> Bless be his great name for evermore!
> For he had scourged me and now
> He has had pity on me and
> I see my son Tobias.

Tobias went into the house, and with a loud voice joyfully blessed God. Then he told his father everything: how his journey had been successful and he had brought the silver back; how he had married Sarah, the daughter of Raguel. Tobit blessed her in these words, "Welcome daughter! Blessed by your God for sending you to us. Blessings on your father, blessings on my son Tobias, and blessings on yourself my daughter. Welcome now to your own house in joyfulness and in blessedness. Come in, my daughter." He held a feast that day for all the Jews of Nineveh to come and share Tobit's happiness.

Chapter 12

When the feasting was over, Tobit called his son Tobias and said, "My son, you ought to think about paying the amount due to your fellow traveler; give him more than the figure agreed upon." "Father," he replied, "how much am I to give him for his help? Even if I give him half the goods he brought back with me, I shall not be the loser. He has brought me back to you safe and sound, he has cured my wife, he has brought the money back too, and now he has cured you as well. How much can I give him for all of this? Tobit said, "He has richly earned half of what he brought back." So Tobias called his companion and said, "Take half of what you brought back, in payment for all you have done, and go in peace."

Then Raphael took them both aside and said, "Bless God, utter his praise before all the living for all the favors he has given you. Bless and extol his name. Proclaim before all men the deeds of God as they deserve, and never tire of giving him thanks. It is right to keep the secret of a king, yet right to reveal and publish the works of God. Thank him worthily. Do what is good, and no evil can befall you.

Prayer with fasting and alms with right conduct are better than riches with impunity. Better to practice almsgiving than to hoard up gold. Almsgiving saves from death and purges every kind of sin. Those who give alms have their fill of days; those who commit sin and do evil, bring harm to themselves.

I am going to tell you the whole truth, hiding nothing from you. I have already told you that it is right to keep the secret of a king, yet right too to reveal in worthy fashion the works of God. So you must know that when you and Sarah were at prayer, it was I who offered you supplications before the glory of the Lord and who read them, so too when you were burying the dead. When you did not hesitate to get up and leave the table to go and bury a dead man, I was sent to test your faith, and at the same time God sent me to heal you and your daughter-in-law Sarah.

I am Raphael, one of seven angels who stand ever ready to enter the presence of the glory of the Lord."

They were both overwhelmed with awe; they fell on their faces in terror. But the angel said, "Do not be afraid; peace be with you. Bless God forever. As far as I was concerned, when I was with you, my presence was not by any decision of mine, but by the will of God; it is he whom you must bless throughout your days, he that you must praise. You thought you saw me eating, but that was appearance and no more. Now bless the Lord on earth and give thanks to God. I am about to return to him who sent me. Write down all that has happened." And he rose in the air.

When they stood up again, he was no longer visible. They praised God with hymns; they thanked him for having performed such wonders;
had not an angel of God appeared to them?

APPENDIX D—THE PEACE AT LAST CONCERT

Peace at Last Inspiration

Peace at Last Concert Invitation 1999–2033

Peace at Last Concert Program 2000

    Introduction

    Old Folks at Home Dvorak/Foster

    Poem by May Angelou (A Brave and Startling Truth)

    Walt Whitman Poetry from Leaves of Grass

    Beautiful Dreamer—Stephen Foster/Imagine John Lennon

Inspiration

On a beautiful summer evening, three and one half billion people from all over the world watched the Olympic representatives of 197 nations marched together for the opening of the 1996 Olympics held in Atlanta, Georgia. The highlights of the pageant were many as Israel, Iran and Iraq all walked in the same parade of champions.

South Africa was accepted back into the games; there was an incredible tribute to my dear comrade, Martin Luther King, Jr.; Celine Dion sang beautifully; and, Muhammad Ali lit the Olympic Flame. I say often we need a universal experience to feel the love and peace of one another and this was one of those times.

The "Peace at Last Concert" to take place at exactly midnight Greenwich Mean time, January 1, 2000 will not have a stadium of spectators, for the stadium will be only an open air spot near the banks of one of the world's rivers. There will not be fireworks, but only one candle will be lit for peace. It will not have expensive sets or costumes, but only one Lily in the spotlight to symbolize the simplicity of peace. As for the music that will be a recording of one of the most beautiful collaborations of 19th century music to be found. That piece is the Stephen Foster song "Old Folks At Home" (know the world over as "Swanee River"), and the Anton Dvorak symphonic choral version of that piece. A Pittsburgh son, and a son of Czechoslovakia offering music to the world as a gift, just like the wonderful "New World Symphony" that Dvorak gave to the United States, and the other 250 songs Stephen Foster left for posterity.

Maybe someday at this Concert, Muhammad Ali would light the candle, Celine Dion would sing the Olympics number, "Awake, Awake" or we would simply just listen and sing along to John Lennon's, "Imagine". Maybe Maya Angelou would give us a poem, as we invite Nobel Peace Prize recipients or their families to recall some of the great peacemakers of all time.

But activity is not the finale. The finale is really in the silence, a beginning and an end, an Alpha and Omega, a Yin and Yang of experience. The experience of Silence.

Together as a world, weary of the battles of life and anxious for an Independence Day of the Spirit, we will breathe out into the Universe as One:

"Peace at Last, Peace at Last, Thank God, for Peace at Last!"

Peace at Last Concert Invitation—2000–2033

Over the last few years organizations such as Peace is Possible Now, the Fellowship of Reconciliation and World Prayer Day have attempted to get the world to unite in a Moment of Silence for the cause of peace. In 1992 this reached the incredible figure of a quarter of a billion people stopping at the exact moment of a New Year's Eve and thinking about peace.

In the year 2000, at exactly twelve midnight Greenwich Mean Time, the world will invite in the Twenty-first century, some will call it the Third Millennium, but we will celebrate that when we bring in the year 2001. On that evening I have planned a concert on the shores of the Swanee River in White Springs, Florida and hope to continue it till my last one before I leave for the stars in 2033.

The musical piece will follow 5 minutes of Silence, and it will first be chimed from the beautiful carillon on the grounds, and then played. It is Stephen Foster's "Old Folks at Home" ("Swanee River") and arranged for chorus and symphony orchestra by Anton Dvorak. The beautiful poem, "A Brave and Startling Truth" by Maya Angelou and a compilation of poetry from Walt Whitman will be read. The program ends with "Imagine" by John Lennon and once again the carillon plays, a Foster Song, "Beautiful Dreamer" as we end in Silence.

As with the 1996 Olympics and the Tribute to Princess Di we look forward to the day when billions of the world's people will share together in a moment of Silence for Peace. The goal after that is for the whole world to join together at once so that we could actually witness the Earth moving closer to the Lawns of Heaven—as the Universe sings out a hymn in the miracle of this Holy Instant:

"Peace at Last, Peace at Last, Thank God for Peace at Last"

The Year 2000 Peace at Last Concert Program
The Swanee River, White Springs Florida
Stephen Foster Memorial and Florida State Park

With the world's attention on the Celebrations going around the globe and fireworks displays of unbelievable and beautiful proportions the clocks have already moved into the 21st century. Greenwich Mean Time used as the Universal time is approaching the Midnight Hour, and here in Florida the time is almost 7:00 PM of the last day of the 20th Century, December 31, 1999.

The Morning Star of the New Day shines upon the Universe and looks on a different world, a world that has been weary and now longs for the attainment of Peace and the Epiphany or Manifestation of the Universal Experience. The world does not need a universal religion, but is does need the Universal Experience. So as the viewers of the world unite in sharing the celebrations of light and music, dance and song, so too do we celebrate coming Home to Peace.

We are its home; its tranquil dwelling place from which it gently reaches out and spreads across the whole of creation. It must begin with one or two, it must begin with us, and from us reach to everyone who calls.

So let us come to this peace place and spend a moment together. Here we share a final dream for peace in the World. As long as thee is a single act of Violence, a single act of War, and as long as a single "Slave" remains to walk the Earth, our release and restoration is not complete.

We are still, and in the Quiet we enter a New Year, a New Century, a new Thousand-Year History, and we realize we share this Universal Experience. We share the music, the poetry, and the moment with the entire world and we realize when we have peace at last we will be Home.

A Moment of Silence for Peace…

> --Five minutes of Silence for Peace throughout the World
> --Carillon playing of "Old Folks at Home" (Swanee River) by Stephen Foster
> --The Antonin Dvorak Choral Symphonic Version of Stephen Foster's "Old Folks at Home (Swanee River) featuring the playing of the 1991 recording by Brazeal Dennard Chorale and

the Civic Orchestra of the Detroit Symphony, Soloist, Samuel McKelton, tenor.
--The Czech Version: "Ten, Jehoz Dum Tu Stal (Swanee River)
The Prague Philharmonic Players and Pavel Kuhn's Male Choir

Good Morning!
We are now into the first moments of the Early morning and the Dawn of a New Century and the first stirrings of the Year 2000.

It is fitting that we begin with words from America's Poet, the wonderful Maya Angelou and in her poem, "On the Pulse of Morning"

And so, we who gather by this tiny but famous river and stand on the Shores of the Swanee, Light a Candle for Peace and gaze upon the Lily of Forgiveness and affirm:
Peace is Possible.
We affirm that the World can make Peace a reality, and that Peace needs to fall upon the Earth like drops of healing rain. Let us continue to believe in the Miracle of Peace.

Our first reading of two is the Poem by Maya Angelou written for the 50th Anniversary of the United Nations. It is called:

<u>*A Brave and Startling Truth*</u>

Our thanks to Maya for such a wonderful poem, and the permission to read it at "The Peace at Last Concert" here is this garden of peace in Florida. The world is Anew, Ascending and spiraling towards Peace.

Our Second Reading like the music of Stephen Foster comes from the 19th century. Walt Whitman addresses himself as he speaks to the Listeners of the Future.
This piece is taken from different poems in his "Leaves of Grass" and I call it:

Walt Whitman's Salute to the World

I chose you Walt because
You are the poet of the future

In this garden the world is
New and ascending.
O to make the most jubilant song!
Full of music, full of
Manhood, womanhood, infancy.

O to realize space!
The plenteousness of all
That there are no bounds
To emerge and be of the sky,
Of the sun and moon and
Flying clouds, as one with them.

The Sun, and stars that float
In the open air
I do not know what it is
Except that it is grand
And that it is happiness.

Whoever you are, the divine ship
Sails the divine sea for you.
Are he or she for whom the
Sun and moon hang in the sky
For none more than you are the
Present and the past
For none more than you is immortality.

I think I could stop here
Myself and do miracles

Why, who makes much of a miracle?
As to me I know nothing else but miracles.
Whether I walk the streets of Manhattan
Or stand under trees in the woods

To me every hour of light and dark is a miracle
The sea, the fishes that swim, the
Motion of the waves, to me,
I know of nothing else but miracles.

Flood-tide below me!
I see you face to face
Just as you are refreshed.
By the gladness of the river
And the bright flow,
I was refreshed.
Flow on River, frolic on!

O take my hand Walt Whitman
Such gliding wonders, such
Sights and Sounds.
What do you see Walt Whitman?
Who are they you salute, and
They one after another who
Salute you?

You whoever you are!
And you of centuries hence
When you listen to me.
Health to you, Good will to
You all, from me and
America sent!

Each of us inevitable—

Each of us limitless—
Each of us with his
Or her right upon the Earth
Each of us here as divinely
As any is here.

My spirit has pass'd in
Compassion and determination
Around the Earth.
I have look'd for
Equals and lovers and have
Found them ready for me
In all lands
I think some divine rapport
Has equalized me with them.

I have taken my stand on
The high embedded roads
And run through all the
Rivers of the globe
To cry
Salut au Monde!
I salute you, O You Wonderful World,
Salut au Monde!

We finish this concert for peace with music as we drift back to the 20th/21st century and listen to John Lennon"s, "Imagine." John saw a world of beautiful children and a world of beautiful dreamers who believed in peace, and truly believed we could live as One. We who know we are not the only ones, listen or sing along with this masterpiece of peace and love.

And as the carillon, here at Stephen Foster State Park, on the shores of the Swanee River, chimes out Stephen Foster's, "Beautiful Dreamer" we return to Silence, and hear an ancient melody playing throughout the Universe. It sighs, it sings, it whispers to a weary world ready for rebirth and joy, a world ready to transform itself into a Bright New World, where the children are safe, and where we offer them this gift of hope. Our every thought joined with one another as our hearts cry out with Joy:

"Peace at Last, Peace at Last, Thank God, for Peace at Last."

0-595-25096-3

Made in the USA
Middletown, DE
29 March 2020